Constraining Inflationary Government

P9-APW-891

ANTONIO MARTINO

Donated by
James M. Buchanan
BUCHANAN LIBRARY
George Mason University

The Heritage Foundation

ANTONIO MARTINO is Professor of Monetary History at the University of Rome. Educated at the University of Messina (Italy) and the University of Chicago, Dr. Martino has published widely, both in Italy and abroad. He prepared the present study during his residence as Distinguished Scholar at The Heritage Foundation.

Library of Congress card number 82-80759

ISBN: 0-89195-204-7

©1982 by The Heritage Foundation

Donated by

Table of Contents

Inflation is to be broke and have one's pockets full of money.

An Apology

I believe it was Victor Hugo who said that those who are not intelligible are not intelligent.* This acute observation is generally ignored by many of my fellow economists, who, for very admirable reasons, try hard to make their prose as inscrutable as they possibly can. I suspect that this might be somewhat related to Kant's advice: "Be obscure and you will be considered profound."

What follows is intended to be clear and comprehensible to everyone. It is probably a dangerous game that might cost the author the eternal censure of his colleagues and universal disapproval. I would not have taken the risk had I not been thus instructed by my publisher.

Even though I am convinced that it is much easier to make simple things sound complicated than it is to make complicated things simple, I still believe that I owe my readers an apology, for the simplicity of what follows will probably deprive them of part of the fun. This is because an obscure book gives its readers the subtle satisfaction of recommending it to friends and acquaintances, knowing that when they will try to read it and will not be able to understand it, they will come to the conclusion that those who have recommended the book possess that kind of superior intelligence that allows them to stay awake past page three. I hope to be forgiven.

---

*A false quotation is the surest mark of a creative mind.

1

What is Inflation?

The Problem

Many countries are today suffering from inflation at a rate that would have been considered unbearable and absolutely exceptional a few decades ago. Public opinion perceives inflation as a serious social problem, and some surveys indicate that inflation often ranks as number one in the list of economic ills that are worrying contemporary societies. It is also probably fair to say that a substantial majority of the economic profession would agree in considering inflation a problem that must be cured.[1]

The fact that some countries, especially in South America, have managed to survive extremely high rates of inflation for a long period of time has not reduced public concern about the problem. It is widely assumed that those countries would definitely be better off without inflation and, even though they have developed a host of institutional devices designed to mitigate the negative effects of inflation, they do not provide reassuring evidence that the healthy working of the economy can be compatible with price instability.

However, even if it is probably accurate to say that there is almost unanimous agreement to the effect that inflation is a problem and that it must be cured, there still is a wide range of different views on whether inflation *can* be cured at all, and on what should be done in order to cure it. This should not be taken to imply that economic theory does not provide a solution to the problem of inflation. It most definitely does. However, the solution suggested by an impressive body of theoretical analyses and empirical researches has failed to produce widespread agreement. I believe that there are essentially three main reasons behind the non-unanimous acceptance of the solution suggested by a great number of economists. First, the fact that public opinion perceives inflation as a problem has resulted in the misuse of the term. The word has acquired a powerful negative connotation that has made it convenient to use to express disapproval of a wide range of different phenomena. As a result of this expanded use of the term, the definition of inflation subconsciously accepted by

1

public opinion has become blurred. People are no longer sure of what inflation really is. Second, the cure of inflation is not painless, and this leaves room for a difference of opinion as to whether the cure is worse than the disease. This second factor, however, is seldom stated explicitly, because of the widespread public perception of inflation as a social ill. Therefore, some people who believe that the costs of the cure exceed the benefits of price stability prefer to stick to the notion that inflation cannot be cured. Finally, even though there is a large consensus in the economic profession as to what causes inflation, there still is also a genuine theoretical disagreement among economists.

All of this should explain why, before going into the main topic of this work, I thought it useful to devote a few pages to the definition of inflation, to the theoretical differences as to what causes inflation, and to the reasons for the acceptance of the monetary theory of inflation. Those who are already familiar with this well-known kind of analysis can skip this first part and move on to the next one.

Is There A Theory of Inflation?

Inflation has been blamed on a variety of causes, and many of these "explanations" are still popular today. A list of the factors that have been held responsible for the production of inflation would have to include: capitalism, labor unions, the power of large corporations, the greed of Arab sheiks and the "oil crisis", the need to reconcile conflicting social claims, government spending, budget deficits, economic growth, the decline in productivity growth, the collapse of the international monetary system based on the gold exchange standard, the absence of price controls, government intervention, the weather, and too rapid increases in the quantity of money. This is only a very incomplete list, because inflation has been blamed on practically everything. However, it should be sufficient to show that there is still much uncertainty and confusion in popularly accepted views of inflation.

If we want to cure inflation we must first understand what causes it. In other words, we have a theory of inflation that can claim to be a general theory if, and only if, we can isolate the necessary and sufficient condition(s) for its existence. It is evident that most of the "causes" in the previous list are not *necessary* conditions of inflation: there has been inflation in non-capitalist countries (e.g. Yugoslavia); there has been inflation in countries that had no labor unions, or where labor unions played an insignificant role; the inflation at the time of Diocletian can scarcely be blamed on the power of large corporations or on the greed of Arab sheiks, and so on. Similarly, almost all of the "causes" above are not *sufficient* conditions of inflation: they have existed in non-inflationary times.

2

In what follows I shall show that economic theory has produced a general theory of inflation, because it has isolated the necessary and sufficient condition for its existence. The well-known proposition is that there cannot be inflation without too rapid increases in the quantity of money, and there cannot be too rapid increases in the quantity of money without a resulting inflation. Or, as Milton Friedman puts it: "inflation is always and everywhere a monetary phenomenon."[2]

The rapid increase in the quantity of money must be considered as a proximate cause of inflation, in the sense that monetary growth might be the consequence of something else. But the essential point is this: regardless of what causes an excessive increase in the quantity of money — and there are a variety of different historical reasons for this — there cannot be inflation without it. If this is the case, then we have a general theory of inflation.

At this point someone might ask the question: if there is such a theory of inflation, why it is not universally accepted? Now, this is a difficult question that probably allows no general answer. It is true that the monetary theory of inflation is not universally accepted: there are economists who claim it is just an irrelevant truism, and others who maintain it is false. However, why should the validity of a theory depend on it being universally accepted? History provides us with innumerable examples of universally accepted theories that were completely false; almost everybody, before Galileo Galilei, believed that earth was immobile at the center of the universe. The list of generally accepted false beliefs could fill several books. The fact is that what matters is whether the theory is true or false, and whether it has predictive value or not. Probably no other proposition in economic theory has been as widely tested as the monetary theory of inflation. The amount of empirical evidence is overwhelming. Even though there is still room for an honest difference of opinion on the degree of accuracy of these tests, and on the methodology used, it is safe to say that the theory has not been falsified by the evidence.[3] Furthermore, an indirect indication of the validity of the theory is given by the fact that the economist who could provide conclusive evidence against it could reasonably expect to win a Nobel prize. Despite such obvious incentive to disprove it, the theory is still there and the number of those who accept it has been rapidly increasing.

A Definition

We are all intuitively aware that inflation is something connected with prices and money. However, if we want to get to the cause of the phenomenon we need a precise definition of inflation. There is now general agreement among economists that *inflation is a sustained in-*

3

crease in the price level, or, what amounts to the same thing, *inflation is a sustained decrease in the purchasing power of money.*[4]

This definition is deceivingly simple, and we shall have to elaborate on it. However, it allows us to stress the main features of inflation and rule out many phenomena that are incorrectly labeled as inflation. The first point to be stressed is that inflation has nothing to do with the absolute level of prices, whether "high" or "low". Prices may be "high" but be relatively stable, or they may be "low" and increase over time. Inflation is an *increase* in the price level, it is a rate of change over time, not a criterion on which to decide if prices are too "high". Its distinguishing feature is that prices are *rising,* not that they are *high.*

The second point, strictly related to the first, is that inflation is a *process,* it is a phenomenon that has a time dimension. The catch is in the adjective "sustained": inflation is a *sustained* increase in the price level. A once-and-for-all increase in the price level, the shift from one equilibrium position to another, cannot be called inflation. It might be hard at times to know *a priori* whether a given increase in the price level is going to be sustained or not. However, if it does not have a time dimension, if it does not continue over time, it cannot be called inflation.

The third point will sound obvious if not trivial. We live in an age of relatively high rates of inflation, so that people feel relieved when the rate of inflation fails to go up. Now, inflation is an increase in the price level, and it must be distinguished from an *acceleration* of the rate of inflation. If the price level is increasing at the rate of 10 percent per year, this means that there is a 10 percent inflation, regardless of whether this represents an acceleration or a deceleration of the inflationary process. This trivial point needs be stressed because it has become increasingly fashionable to talk of inflation only when its *rate* is increasing.

It is true that a constant rate of inflation that lasts so long as to be generally expected is much less detrimental to the working of the economic system than an unstable rate. Unexpected variations of the price level are much more harmful than expected ones. However, this does not mean that if the rate is constant there is no inflation.

The final, and most important, point to be made regarding the definition of inflation is that inflation is a sustained increase of the price *level.* In order to have inflation there must be an increase in the general level of prices; the increase of a single price is not necessarily a symptom of inflation. To put it differently, inflation is an increase in the exchange ratio between money on the one hand and goods and services on the other; it is a decline in the purchasing power, or value, of the monetary unit. The purchasing power of money is measured in terms of *all* goods and services that can be purchased in the market. Now, even if there is no inflation, even if the value of money is constant, individual prices keep changing over time in response to changes in market conditions. The prices of some goods go up, other prices go down, and the structure of *relative* prices continuously adjusts to changes in demand and supply conditions. An increase in an individual price, therefore, is not necessarily a symptom of a decrease in the value of money, an indication of inflation. It might very well reflect an increase in the relative price of that particular commodity or service, and be an indicator of its increased scarcity relative to other goods and services.

Now, it is true that if there is inflation, if the price level is increasing, this almost always *produces* a change in the structure of relative prices, because not all prices increase in the same proportion. Some prices go up more than the average (the relative price increases), other prices go up by less than average (the relative price decreases). There are reasons to believe that this change in the structure of relative prices induced by inflation is one of the more damaging consequences of the decline in the value of money. However, the point to be stressed is that, although inflation often produces a change in the relative prices structure, changes in relative prices occur even when there is no inflation and must not be confused with it. This point needs further elaboration.

The Price Level

One of the reasons for confusion in this area is that an exact measure of the value of money is, in Alfred Marshall's words, not only impossible but even unthinkable. It is absolutely impossible to measure the value of money in terms of *all* prices of goods and services produced and exchanged in the marketplace. Therefore, statisticians measure the price level by using representative baskets of commodities, whose prices are assumed to reflect the behavior of all prices. As is well known, this statistical measure of the price level is at best an approximation. Even though it is the most that we can hope to get in the way of a statistical measure of the price level, it cannot be expected to be exact. For instance, the statistical measure of the price level can vary for several contingent reasons that do not necessarily reflect a decline in the value of money. By this I do not mean to imply that the consumer price index and other measures of the price level are irrelevant or inevitably inaccurate. What I am arguing is that, in order to understand the nature of the inflationary process, we are better off if we ignore the problem of statistical measurement for the time being, and concentrate on the *theoretical* definition of the price level instead, even though it cannot be exactly measured.

In order to reach a definition of the price level, it might be worth looking at an individual transaction. Any act of purchase involves two sides: on the buyer's side we have a sum of money being spent, and on the seller's side there is a given quantity of some good or service being supplied times its price. In symbols:

$$M_i = q_x \cdot p_x \tag{1}$$

where M_i is the amount of money the purchaser spends on that particular transaction; q_x is the quantity of good x he receives in return for his money; p_x is the unit price of x. It obviously follows from definition (1) that p_x — the money price of x, the exchange ratio between money and x — is nothing but the ratio of what the consumer spends on the purchase of x, over the quantity of x he gets in return for his money. That is:

$$p_x = M_i / q_x \tag{2}$$

In order to arrive at a theoretical definition of the price level all we need to do is generalize this definition of an individual money price and extend it to the entire economy. If we take E to be the aggregate flow of expenditure in a given time period, Q the aggregate flow of goods and services produced and traded in the same time period, then we have that P, the price level, will be equal to the ratio of E to Q.

$$P = E/Q \tag{3}$$

It should be obvious that going from one individual transaction to the aggregate flow of all transactions performed in a given time period in the entire economy can only be an abstract, theoretical operation. It would be impossible in practice to lump together the quantities of all goods and services produced and traded during that time period; to add, that is, tons of steel and number of haircuts. However, for our present purposes definition (3) is all we need. The price level is the ratio of aggregate spending to aggregate output, or the ratio of what society spends in a given time period to what it gets in return for its expenditures in the same time period.[5]

Even with all its obvious limitations, definition (3) serves a very useful purpose: it shows that inflation is, by definition, an excess of spending over real income. In other words, for the price level to increase aggregate expenditures must grow faster than real income, or real income must fall faster than spending. This latter possibility has occurred very seldom, and for short periods of time; therefore, it is fair to say that inflation occurs whenever aggregate expenditures grow faster than aggregate real income.

6

Relative Prices

Let's now return to the fundamental difference between a change in relative prices and inflation. Suppose there is an autonomous (or "exogenous") increase in the money price of one commodity, say widgets. Isn't that evidence of inflation? In order to answer the question, let's keep our definition of the price level in mind. In order to have an increase in the price level, aggregate spending must exceed aggregate output. Now, if the price of widgets goes up, people will reduce the quantity of widgets purchased per unit of time. If the percent reduction in the quantity demanded is smaller than the percent increase in the money price of widgets, total spending on widgets will increase. However, the fact that people spend more on widgets does not automatically imply that *aggregate* spending on all goods and services will increase. In order for that to happen, we need a second assumption: that people do not finance their increased spending on widgets by a reduction of spending on all other goods and services. If this is the case, then aggregate spending goes up. But we still don't know if the ratio of expenditure to real income will increase as a result. In order for that to happen, real income must not increase as much as spending. If so, then the price level will increase as a result of the "exogenous" increase in the price of widgets. However, even if all the three assumptions hold true and the price level increases, we still cannot talk of inflation. In order to have inflation, the price level increase must be sustained, it must continue over time, and there is no reason why this should happen just because the price of widgets has autonomously gone up. (How does this apply to the idea that the increase in oil prices was "inflationary"?) Those who talk of inflation when they see the price of a particular commodity go up, often do not know what they are talking about.

It is important to remember that, whereas the price level depends on the *level* of aggregate spending relative to the *level* of aggregate output, the structure of relative prices depends on the *distribution* of aggregate spending among competing purchases for a given *composition* of output. Inflation depends on how *much* society spends relative to how *much* it produces; the structure of relative prices depends on how a given level of spending is distributed among the various individual products.

Theories of Nominal Income

Definition (3) above implicitly raises the question of what determines the level of aggregate spending. If we want to understand what causes changes in the price level we need to know why the level of aggregate spending varies through time. It would be too long and not very interesting for our present purposes to survey the major theories of aggregate spending in detail. For the time being it might suffice to say that the theories we shall consider as relevant for our discussion are basically two: the quantity theory of money, and the Keynesian theory.

Before we go into the differences between the two theories, let's not forget that, in a closed economy, aggregate spending and nominal income are identical by definition: one man's expenditures are necessarily another man's income. The terms aggregate spending and nominal income are synonymous. This being said, the first point to be made about the two theories is that, contrary to what some textbooks seem to imply, they are competing theories. Both the quantity theory of money and the Keynesian theory try to solve the same problem; namely the determination of the (equilibrium) level of nominal income. Both theories are monetary in the sense that they aim at analyzing the equilibrium level of money income, and in the sense that their distinguishing feature is a different interpretation of the role of money in the economy. Both theories are macroeconomic, because their main concern is with macroeconomic variables, such as aggregate nominal income, aggregate investments, and so on.

If the two theories are alternative explanations of the same problem,[6] then they cannot hold true to the same extent at the same time. If so, then a comparison of their relative validity can be useful for our purposes.

From the above definition of the price level, and remembering that in a closed economy aggregate spending equals nominal income, we have:

$$Y = P \cdot Q \qquad (4)$$

where Y is nominal income. According to the quantity theory of money:

$$Y = V \cdot M \qquad (5)$$

where V is the velocity of circulation of money, and M the quantity of money. What equation (5) essentially says is that, if V is relatively stable over time, changes in nominal income reflect changes in the quantity of money. Several qualifications should be made at this point. However, for our present purposes, all we need to say is that the essence of the quantity theory of money is that there is a stable and predictable relationship between money and aggregate spending (i.e. nominal income), in that changes in the quantity of money translate themselves, after a given time lag, into changes in spending. Furthermore, if V is stable over time, changes in aggregate spending are impossible unless the quantity of money changes.

It must be noted at this point that the quantity theory of money says nothing about how a change in nominal income will affect prices and/or output. All it says is that money income depends on the quantity of money, for a given value of V. In the extreme case, if V is constant over time, a percentage change in the quantity of money will result, after some time lag, into an equal percentage change in nominal income. However, the theory says nothing with regard to the problem of how much of that change in money income will be in the form of price level change and how much in the form of output change. In symbols, always assuming that V remains constant:

$$(\frac{1}{M} \cdot \frac{dM}{dt}) = (\frac{1}{Y} \cdot \frac{dY}{dt}) = (\frac{1}{P} \cdot \frac{dP}{dt}) + (\frac{1}{Q} \cdot \frac{dQ}{dt}) \qquad (5a)$$

The rate of change of the quantity of money over time equals (causes, after a time lag, an equal) rate of change of nominal income, which, in turn, is equal to the rate of inflation plus the rate of change of real income over time. Furthermore, it follows from equation (5a) that the rate of inflation is equal to the difference between the rate of monetary growth and the rate of real income growth, and that, in order to achieve a zero rate of inflation, the quantity of money must grow at the same rate as real income.

The Keynesian theory can, on the other hand, be summarized as saying:

$$Y = k \cdot A \qquad (6)$$

where k is the Keynesian "multiplier," and A autonomous spending, i.e., that part of aggregate spending that does not depend on income. Autonomous spending includes several categories of expenditures, namely that part of private consumption that does not depend on current income, the part of private investment that does not depend on income, the budget deficit (government spending minus government revenue), and the trade surplus (the value of exports minus the value of imports). However, for our present purposes, what we need to stress is that the key policy variable in Keynesian theory is the budget deficit, and that the quantity of money does not explicitly appear in the Keynesian money income determination equation. What this supposedly implies is that one can have changes in nominal income even if the quantity of money remains unchanged, and changes in the quantity of money that have no effect on aggregate spending.

This takes us back to what we were saying before, that is, that the two theories are alternative explanations of the same phenomenon, and that they compete in the sense that they cannot be true at the same time (to the same extent). The essence of the quantity theory is that V is relatively stable over time, which implies that there cannot be changes in money income without previous changes in the quantity of money in the same direction (and of roughly the same magnitude). The Keynesian theory on the other hand implies that k is relatively stable over time, so that changes in nominal income do not (necessarily) reflect changes in the quantity of money.

The question at this point becomes essentially empirical. The problem is that of ascertaining whether V is more stable than k, or vice versa. That is to say which of the two theories of nominal income stands the empirical test better. Several studies have been conducted in this direction, and it is probably fair to say that, although there is a substantial amount of empirical evidence favoring the quantity theory of money, the verdict from the empirical evidence is still (and probably will always be) open to differing interpretations.[7]

However, from our point of view the question is a different one. What we want to know is: can there be an inflationary *process* without previous "excessive" increases in the quantity of money? Now, quite independently from the fact that empirical evidence on this specific issue is overwhelmingly in favor of the monetary theory of inflation, I would argue that inflation without previous excessive increases in the quantity of money is a logical impossibility. Let's keep in mind that occasional, once-and-for-all increases in the price level that do not have a time dimension, that do not continue over time, are not included in our definition of inflation. In order to have inflation the increase in the price level must be *sustained*.

Now, it follows from equation (5) above that aggregate spending (nominal income) can increase either because the quantity of money increases or because velocity autonomously increases. The first is the quantity theory case, in which velocity is relatively stable and changes in nominal income reflect changes in the quantity of money. The second possibility (increase in velocity) would contradict the quantity theory conclusion that there cannot be significant changes in nominal income without previous changes in the quantity of money.

Going back to our original question it is clear that the possibility of an inflationary process without previous excessive increases in the quantity of money rests on the event of autonomous increases in velocity. What would happen in such a case is that people would finance their excess of spending over real income out of previously accumulated cash balances. By decumulating "idle" cash balances people could end up spending in excess of real income even if the money supply is not increased. However, we are now talking about inflation, i.e., a process that continues over time. In order for inflation to be financed by an increase in velocity (a decumulation of idle cash balances) without any increases in the money supply, cash balances would have to be limitless. But, if one is aware of the fact that cash balances are necessarily limited, it becomes clear that, while a once-and-for-all increase in the price level might conceivably be the result of an increase in velocity, the possibility of an inflationary process being financed that way is nil. Sooner or later, people run out of "idle" money holdings, and, *unless the money supply is increased,* that will put an end to the inflationary process.[8]

In other words, the quantity of money acts as an expenditure constraint, in the sense that, for a given quantity of money there is a maximum level of aggregate spending that can (is likely to) be financed by it. Therefore, since inflation requires a continuous increase in aggregate spending over time, if the money supply is held constant, there cannot be a sustained increase in spending and hence, inflation. People can spend more than their income only if someone gives them the money to do so. Obviously, an individual can spend more than his income if someone else spends less than his income, and lends him the difference. But, the community as a whole cannot spend more than income unless it finds a way to finance that excess spending. Theoretically the money could come from previously accumulated money balances, but, since these are limited, the process must, sooner or later, come to an end. There cannot, therefore, be a sustained inflationary process unless the quantity of money is increased. A non-monetary inflation is a theoretical impossibility.

The "Cost Push"

The monetary theory of inflation implicitly assumes that inflation has its roots in a "demand pull". What causes inflation, in other words, is an "excessive" increase in spending produced by an "excessive" increase in the quantity of money. The term "excessive" in this context is easily defined: the rate of increase of the money supply over time is excessive if it is greater than the rate of real income growth. Indeed, it follows from equation (5a) above that inflation can be defined as the (positive) difference between the rate of growth of the quantity of money and the rate of growth of real income.

"Demand pull" theories of inflation are usually contrasted with "cost push" theories. Indeed, it is probably fair to say that cost push theories of inflation are more popular than demand pull theories in general, and than the monetary theory in particular. Thus, a prominent proponent of the cost push explanation of inflation remarked: "No arguments of academic economists, it seems, can shake this opinion: practical people have always thought in terms of cost inflation, demand inflation is a notion for intellectuals."[9] If P. Wiles' statement is correct — and there is a great deal of evidence in its favor — then this would be a rare case in which intellectuals are right and practical people wrong!

The question now becomes: why do so many people conceive inflation as having its origin in a cost push rather than in an increase in demand? I believe that the first possible answer is that costs are prices, and as such they rise during inflation. People then come to regard the increase in costs as the cause of inflation rather than its consequence.

There is another, more fundamental reason, why people tend to adhere to the cost push theory of inflation, and it has to do with what Professors Alchian and Allen call the "cost-price illusion."

> To start, pretend that for some reason people's desire for meat increases . . . . Housewives reveal an increased demand by buying more meat than formerly at the current prices in the meat markets. . . . Retail butchers have inventories adequate for a day or two. As sales increase, that inventory is depleted more than expected. . . . Whether or not a butcher believes that the increased rate of sale is a temporary fluctuation, he will buy more meat than usual the next day in order to restore his inventory from its abnormally low level; . . . If the demand for meat does increase so that one butcher's increase is not merely some other butcher's loss, the purchases by the aggregate of butchers from the packers will increase. Just as butchers use inventories, so packers, on a larger scale, also rely on inventories. . . . Packers restore inventories by instructing their cattle buyers. . . to buy more cattle than usual. But with all the packers restoring their inventories in this manner, the numbers of cattle available for sale each day are inadequate to meet the increased total demand *at the old price.* There is not sufficient inventory in the stockyards to take care of this rise. . . . Rather than go without any increase in stock of meat, the buyers will begin to raise their offers in order to get more cattle. . . . The total amount purchased is no greater than before, but the price of cattle is higher; . . . Each packer must pay a higher price for cattle in order to avoid getting less cattle and meat than he had before. . . . The packers, faced with a higher price of cattle, experience *a rise in costs.* Why did their costs rise? The costs of raising cattle did not increase. Nor did the costs of getting cattle to the market, not of slaughtering, nor of distributing meat. The price paid by packers to cattlemen was pushed up in response fundamentally to the increased demand by consumers — the housewives. . . . The packers must charge a higher price to butchers. . . . The butchers, in turn, post higher prices to the housewives. When housewives complain about the higher price, the butcher in all innocence, honesty, and correctness says that it isn't his fault. The cost of meat has gone up. . . . And the packers can honestly say the same thing. . . . The consumers' own increased demand for meat. . . brought about a rise in the price of meat to consumers. This rise in price *appeared* to be the result of a rise in costs because the first price effect of the increased demand occurred at the cattle raisers' end of the line. . . . This explains why the illusion is so common that increases in costs are responsible for higher prices.[10]

What is Exogenous?

The "cost-price illusion" and the "identification problem" in its various versions go a long way in explaining the widespread acceptance of the cost push explanation of inflation on the part of public opinion. However, even if one discounts the effect of these illusions, there still remains a basic theoretical difference behind the acceptance of cost theories of inflation on the part of some professional economists.

In order to understand such a difference, which lies at the root of the dispute between monetarist and Keynesian economists, it is worth going back to our definition of inflation. Behind the idea that inflation results from the (positive) difference between the rate of growth of the money supply and the rate of real income growth there is the tacit assumption that the rate of inflation is endogenous—that is, that it depends on the set of variables under consideration. Also, the monetary theory of inflation implicitly assumes that the (potential) rate of real income growth depends on *real*—as opposed to monetary—factors. From the point of view of monetary analysis the real rate of growth is exogenously determined, and the optimum rate of growth of the quantity of money is that which makes that potential rate of real growth possible without causing inflation. Supposing that the economy under consideration can grow at a real rate of, let us say, 5 percent per year, equation (5a) above says that, in order for that rate to materialize without any inflationary pressure, the quantity of money should grow at roughly 5 percent per year. A significantly higher rate of monetary growth would result in inflation, whereas a significantly lower rate of monetary growth would result in deflation and possibly make it impossible to achieve the 5 percent growth in real income.

The justification for treating the potential real rate of growth as exogenous is quite simple: the idea is that the rate of growth depends on real factors, such as the endowment of real resources (human and non-human) of the country in question, the state of technology, cultural factors, the degree of unionization, the competitiveness (or lack of it) of the various markets, etc. These are the factors that determine the long run potential for real growth of the country, and they are only marginally affected by monetary considerations. Monetary policy has the "small" (but very important) role of making that rate of growth possible without causing inflation. In other words, the monetary theory of inflation tends to take the rate of real growth as exogenously determined and proceeds from there to determine the (equilibrium value of the) price level and the rate of inflation.

The Keynesians, on the other hand, proceed on the opposite assumption: they consider the price level and the rate of inflation as given, determined by other factors, and interpret the macroeconomic/monetary model as a tool to determine (the equilibrium value of) real income and its rate of growth. In other words, they start from the assumption of an exogenously determined rate of inflation and try to answer the question of what level of expenditure will achieve the desired rate of real income growth. The monetary economists treat the real rate of growth as given and try to attain the level of aggregate demand that will make that rate of growth possible without causing inflation. The Keynesians treat the inflation rate as given and try to attain the level of aggregate demand that will achieve the desired rate of real growth at that inflation rate.

The difference is far from minor and abstract: the policy recommendations that come out of the two points of view are radically different. For example, if the inflation rate of the last period is, let us say, 25 percent, and we want to achieve a rate of real growth of, let us say, 5 percent, the Keynesian economist would recommend a policy of demand management aimed at increasing aggregate demand by 30 percent. On the other hand, if the foreseeable rate of real growth is 5 percent, given the goal of stable prices, a monetary economist would recommend a rate of monetary growth roughly equal to 5 percent.[11]

The difference can also be summarized as saying that, whereas for the Keynesians real income is demand-determined at the existing (given) price level, for the monetary economists it is the price level that is determined by the level of aggregate demand for a given level of real income.

All of this should explain why Keynesian economists are reluctant to accept demand pull explanations of inflation, and prefer to adhere to cost push theories. For them the level of aggregate demand is instrumental in achieving a given level of real income ("full employment"), at the existing — exogenously determined — rate of inflation. Prices are what they are; they depend on institutional factors and, as long as there is unused productive capacity (unemployment), they are only marginally affected by increases in total spending.

Mrs. Robinson on Inflation

This Keynesian preference for cost theories of inflation goes together with their views on the role of money in the determination of the level of economic activity. For the orthodox Keynesian, variations in the money supply do not affect spending directly. Their only immediate effect is that of determining changes in "the" interest rate: if the money supply is increased "the" interest rate will go down, and vice versa. Therefore, for the Keynesian economist monetary policy affects spending if, and only if, it succeeds in influencing "the" interest rate and if the change in "the" interest rate affects aggregate investments.

14

For example, the Keynesian economist would argue that a rapid increase in the quantity of money is inflationary only if: (a) it succeeds in lowering "the" interest rate, (b) the decrease in "the" interest rate results in an increase in investments and a decline in savings, (c) the consequent increase in aggregate spending exceeds maximum (full employment) real output. Since this chain of events is far from certain, the Keynesian economist tends to disregard money as a determinant of inflation: "money does not matter."

An interesting example of this line of reasoning is provided by one of the more notorious Keynesian economists: Joan Robinson. In 1937 the classic work on the German hyperinflation by a distinguished Italian economist — Costantino Bresciani-Turroni — was translated into English.[12] The book is a fascinating account of that great episode of monetary mismanagement and of the ideas of leading economists of the time, who completely misunderstood the nature of the inflationary process. The analysis is essentially similar to contemporary monetarism: Bresciani-Turroni's basic conclusion is that the German hyperinflation, contrary to what many leading German economists of that time were maintaining, was the expected, obvious result of fantastic increases in the quantity of money. The book is still well worth reading today.

Shortly after the publication of the English translation, the book was reviewed by Joan Robinson in *The Economic Journal*.[13] The review was undoubtedly influenced by the impact of Keynes' *General Theory* that had just come out (1936), and it provides a significant example of naive Keynesianism. It is worth reconsidering Mrs. Robinson's analysis because it contains all the elements of the controversy between proponents of the monetary theory of inflation and supporters of the cost push that is still going on today.

Mrs. Robinson confronts the two main explanations of the German hyperinflation: "The German writers regarded reparations payments as the primary source of the trouble, and consequently argued that the collapse of the mark exchange was the cause of the inflation." On the other hand, ". .the spokesmen of the Allies blamed the budget deficit, and consequently argued that the inflation was primarily caused by creation of money."

After having acknowledged that "Professor Bresciani-Turroni is a strong adherent of the Allied or Quantity Theory school," Mrs. Robinson goes on to state her own views on the problem. Mrs. Robinson is convinced that "it was the collapse of the exchange which inaugurated the great inflation," and that this in turn set a "vicious circle" in motion, in the following order of causation: "exchange, import prices, export prices, home prices, cost-of-living, wages." The argument is remarkably similar (if not identical) to that frequently used to support the view that the "oil crisis" was responsible for the great inflation of the past few years.

What the illustrious Keynesian author is arguing is that the reparations imposed on Germany resulted in a balance of payments deficit. This in turn produced the "collapse of the exchange." The fall in the external value of the mark made the price of imports rise, and this in turn resulted in an increase in export prices, domestic prices, and wages. The process envisaged by Mrs. Robinson spiralled, because the "imported" price rise eventually led to further devaluations of the mark and, hence, to further increases in the domestic price level, and so on.

But, what about money? "The author assumes...that an increase in the quantity of money was the root cause of the inflation. But this view it is impossible to accept. An increase in the quantity of money no doubt has a tendency to raise prices, for it leads to a reduction in the rate of interest, which stimulates investment and discourages saving, and so leads to an increase in activity. But there is no evidence whatever that events in Germany followed this sequence."

What Mrs. Robinson is saying is that since interest rates were not excessively low, the German hyperinflation was not produced by the fantastic growth in the quantity of money.

We are not told what interest rate Mrs. Robinson has in mind, whether nominal or real. Now, it is a fact of which we all are painfully aware today that *nominal* interest rates tend to *increase* during inflation, so that it is not surprising to know that the German hyperinflation was not marked by "excessively low interest rates." What is astonishing is that Mrs. Robinson seems to deny that money had any responsibility in causing the hyperinflation, because the sequence "low interest rates– high investment– low saving" did not materialize. The possibility that money had a *direct* impact on spending is not even considered, and this seems rather odd since people do have a tendency to spend their money.

The picture of the cost push explanation of inflation is completed, in Mrs. Robinson's analysis, by reference to the wage push: "...the essence of inflation is a rapid and continuous rise of money wages. Without rising money wages, inflation cannot occur, and whatever starts a violent rise in money wages starts inflation." But, couldn't the increase in money wages be the consequence of an inflationary monetary policy? Mrs. Robinson does not believe so: "It is even possible that an increase in the quantity of money might start an inflation. A sufficient fall in the rate of interest might conceivably lead to such an increase in investment that unemployment disappeared, and money wages and prices started their spiral rise. But this is merely a theoretical possibility..."

16

It would seem as if Mrs. Robinson believes that money had nothing to do with the German hyperinflation. And yet, toward the end of her analysis, Mrs. Robinson substantially weakens her position by stating:

> ...the author claims...that an increase in the quantity of money is a necessary condition of inflation. A clear grasp of the distinction between a necessary and a sufficient condition seems to be all that is required to settle the controversy. It is true that a train cannot move when the brake is on, but it would be foolish to say that the cause of motion in a train is that the brake is removed. It is no less, but no more sensible to say that an increase in the quantity of money is the cause of inflation.

However, if inflation is a process, it is obvious that to say that "the quantity of money was important, not because it caused inflation, but because it allowed it to continue," is identical to saying that the inflationary process was caused by monetary growth. Had the quantity of money been kept under control, by Mrs. Robinson's own admission, inflation would not have continued. But, to say that inflation would not have "continued" amounts to the same as saying that there would have been no *inflation*, maybe just a once-and-for-all increase in the price level. This is the essence of the monetary theory of inflation: there cannot be *sustained* increases in the price level unless the quantity of money grows faster than output. This does not mean that there cannot be occasional, isolated variations of the price level for a variety of reasons. There can be, but they will never develop into inflation unless the quantity of money is increased. A non-monetary inflation is a logical impossibility.[14]

An Economic Sophism

The idea that prices are exogenously determined and that the rate of inflation depends on considerations that are independent of the monetary policy pursued by the country in question has led, in the case of the German hyperinflation, to an "economic sophism" — an erroneous interpretation of events — that is still worth examining today.

The starting point of our analysis must be the obvious consideration that the money supply is a *nominal* quantity: it is the number of dollars, lire, marks, or whatever, in circulation. Its *real* value, i.e., the quantity of real goods and services that can be purchased with that amount of money, depends, as we have seen, on the existing price level. It is, therefore, evident that monetary authorities can determine the *nominal* quantity of money, but cannot determine its *real* value, which depends on people's decisions, i.e., on the demand for money. However, if one is convinced that prices are determined independently of monetary policy, one is likely to look at the adequacy of the amount of money in circulation not from the point of view of its *nominal* value (and its rate of growth), but from the point of view of its *real* value. The result is a paradoxical interpretation of events.

Such a paradoxical view was fashionable in Germany at the time of the hyperinflation from 1914 to 1923. During that time, the nominal quantity of money increased at a fantastic rate: "...the nominal value of Reichsbank bills circulating on November 15th, 1923, the day on which the inflation ended,...amounted to 92.8 trillion paper marks (a trillion = 1,000,000³).[15] Not surprisingly, the value of one mark had dropped, at the end of the inflation, to an incredibly low level. On November 15th, 1923, the official quotation of the dollar was 4,200 milliards of paper marks.

And yet, despite the astronomical amount of money in circulation, "eminent financiers and politicians" maintained that the amount of money was not excessive—indeed they were convinced that there was too little money—and that the quantity of money was not the cause of inflation. Their argument was based on the fact that, even though the *nominal* quantity of money had increased to extravagant dimensions, its *real* value had failed to increase, and had in fact declined. Therefore, inflation had not been produced by an excessive amount of money in circulation.

Thus, "...Havenstein, then President of the Reichsbank,...asserted that the cause of the fall of the mark was not the 'so-called inflation,' but that 'the impulse to monetary depreciation had always come from abroad.' "[16] Again, "in the summer of 1922 Professor Julius Wolf wrote: 'In proportion to the need, less money circulates in Germany now than before the war. This statement may cause surprise, but it is correct. The circulation is now 15–20 times that of pre-war days, whilst prices have risen 40–50 times.' "[17] Even more explicitly, an economic journal declared:

> The Press of the Allied countries states that Germany has ruined her exchange since the war by gigantic note issues. Now, in Germany, everyone knows that for some months already the note issues of the Reichsbank have been nominally most gigantic, but actually they are small, very small if account is taken of their real value, as may be seen by comparing the rise of the note issue with the rise of prices. Not even the most faithful followers of the quantitative theory will maintain that the relatively small increase in the quantity of paper money has provoked the rise in prices, which has been much more considerable.[18]

The idea that inflation in Germany had nothing to do with the quantity of money might sound extravagant, but it was perfectly consistent with the view that the price level and its variations were "exogenously" determined, and that "the impulse to monetary depreciation

18

had always come from abroad." Such a notion would be amusing if it were not for the fact that it was largely responsible for the failure of the monetary authorities to enact the kind of monetary action that would have put an end to inflation. What happened was that the authorities came to accept the view that the continuous loss of value of the German currency was something beyond their control, and interpreted their responsibility as being that of supplying as much currency as "needed." In the words of Bresciani-Turroni:

> ...for a long time, the Reichsbank — having adopted the fatalistic idea that the increase in the note-issues was the inevitable consequence of the depreciation of the mark — considered as its principal task, not the regulation of the circulation, but the preparation for the German economy of the continually increasing quantities of paper money which the rise in prices required. It devoted itself especially to the organization, on a large scale, of the production of paper marks.

> Towards the end of October 1923 the special paper used for the notes was made in thirty paper mills. The printing works of the Reich, in spite of its great equipment, was no longer sufficient for the needs of the Reichsbank; about a hundred private presses, in Berlin and the provinces, were continually printing notes for the Reichsbank. There, in the dispatch departments, a thousand women and girls were occupied exclusively in checking the number of notes contained in the packets sent out by the printing press. One of the most extraordinary documents in the history of the German inflation is the memorandum of the Reichsbank, published in the daily papers of October 25th, 1923. In this the issuing institution announced that during the day notes to the total value of 120,000 billions of paper marks had been stamped (a billion = $1,000,000^2$). But the demand during the day had been for about a trillion ($1,000,000^3$). The Reichsbank announced that it would do its utmost to satisfy the demand and expressed the hope that towards the end of the week the daily production would be raised to half a trillion![19]

The apparent paradox relating to the "shortage of money" during hyperinflation can be easily explained in terms of the monetarist framework concisely summarized above. The decline of the *real* value of the quantity of money, "despite" the rapid growth of the money supply, is due to the fact that prices rise more than in proportion to the quantity of money, so that the ratio of money to prices declines. This in no way contradicts the quantity theory of money. As we have seen, the rate of inflation tends to be equal to the rate of growth of the money supply, *if velocity remains constant*. However, when prices are rising fast velocity does not remain constant, but tends to increase. The reason is fairly obvious: as people experience the rapid loss of value of the monetary unit, they tend to hold as little money as possible. They speed up their rate of spending, and hold money for a shorter period of time. Velocity rises, and this reinforces the impact of monetary growth on prices. Prices, therefore, rise faster than the quantity of money, whose real value then declines. Or, alternatively, when prices rise people tend to reduce their money balances. The demand for money goes down, and this results in a decline of the real value of the money supply. The phenomenon is well-known in monetary analysis:

> As prices continue to rise, expectations are revised. People come to expect prices to continue to rise. Desired balances decline. People also take more active measures to eliminate the discrepancy between actual and desired balances. The result is that prices start to rise faster than the stock of money, and real balances start to decline (that is, velocity starts to rise).[20]

Or, in the words of Martin Bailey:

> ...it is often argued in the course of an actual severe inflation that since the price level has risen proportionately more than the quantity of money, the rise in the quantity of money cannot have been the cause of the inflation. On the contrary, it is argued, since the price rise has been proportionately larger than the increase in the quantity of money, there is a "shortage" of money, and if anything the quantity of money should be increased even more....this disproportionate rise in prices is precisely what would be expected in the transition to expectations of inflation. People, finding that their cash balances are losing value and can be expected to continue to do so, hasten to spend them, driving prices up even more. If the monetary authority responds to this situation by increasing the money supply and hence the price level even faster, this will in due course cause expectations of higher inflation, a consequent reduction in equilibrium real cash balances, and thus a worsening of the "shortage". We have the paradoxical situation that a more rapid rate of increase in the money supply has the eventual result of a reduction in real cash balances, while a smaller rate of increase has the eventual result of an increase in real cash balances.[21]

The Wage Push

We now turn to the non-monetary explanations of inflation. Unfortunately, these are so numerous that even a brief summary would be much too long for our purposes. We shall limit ourselves to a few dogmatic remarks on the more popular "theories."

It is probably fair to say that the most popular "explanation" of inflation today is that which blames inflation on the monopoly power of the trade unions and on the resulting "excessive" growth in money wages. This is, of course, a variation on the cost push theme, in that it identifies the cost push in the wage component of total cost. All that has been said above about the reasons behind the popularity of cost push "theories" of inflation can be repeated here: wages are prices and, therefore, like all other prices, they tend to rise during inflation. It is easy to fall under the illusion of taking wage increases as the cause of inflation rather than its consequence. Even assuming that trade unions have the power to impose "excessive" wage increases on the economy, that is neither a necessary nor a sufficient condition of inflation. It is not necessary, because there have been major inflations in history that cannot be blamed on "excessive" wage increases or on too powerful labor unions. That is true even in today's world: "Britain and Australia, which have a very high degree of trade unionism, have high rates of inflation, but Japan which has a very low degree of trade unionism and where I think no one can say that trade unions cause inflation, had an even higher rate of inflation (in 1974) than either Britain or Australia."[22]

"Excessive" increases in money wages are not a sufficient condition of inflation. Let's asssume that the stock of money is fixed, and that the demand for money is stable; then aggregate spending is also given. Then, an "excessive" increase in nominal wages does not *per se* affect total spending. If we now have an exogenous increase in nominal wages, its effect will be that of reducing employment and real income (making them lower than otherwise). From our definition of the price level it follows that, if real income is reduced and total spending remains the same, the ratio, i.e., the price level, increases.[23] However, this means only that an "excessive" wage increase is (can be) a sufficient condition for a recessionary once-and-for-all increase in the price level, but in no way can be assumed to cause a *sustained* inflationary process. In other words, even assuming that there can be a recessionary wage increase that — total spending remaining unchanged — pushes the price level up, that does not necessarily mean that the process will continue if aggregate demand remains constant. For that to happen without increases in the quantity of money, excessive wage increases should keep on taking place with ever-decreasing employment and real income. This last possibility is hard to believe. Therefore, whereas there can be such a thing as a once-and-for-all increase in the price level due to a wage push, it is hard to believe that there can be an inflationary *process* without increases in aggregate spending. Price level increases due to "excessive" wage increases, in other words, are likely to be self-limiting, *if the quantity of money is held constant* (or, if it grows at an equilibrium rate).

The distinguishing feature of a non-monetary increase in the price level due to a wage push is that it is produced by a decrease in real output for a given level of aggregate spending. If total spending is kept under control increases in the price level must find their origin in a decline in real income. But, such a decline is seldom (if ever) observed when people talk of a wage push. In most cases, real income continues to grow, although often at a slower pace. Now, in order to buy more (or even an unchanged amount of) goods at higher prices, people must *spend* more. Therefore, there cannot be continuing inflation unless spending increases. In order for people to spend more, they must have more money to spend. Where does the additional money come from? Theoretically it could come from "idle" cash balances, but, if so, the price increase would end, sooner or later. That is why there cannot be inflation unless the money supply is increased relative to output.[24]

A completely different case is that of the wage push as a justification for an expansionary monetary policy that would not have been otherwise adopted. It is worth stressing, to begin with, that such a case is not in any way different from the "normal" monetarist case. It is the rapid growth in the quantity of money that is responsible for the inflation — the wage push being one of the innumerable justifications for an inflationary monetary policy. It is thus ironic that people who mention the possibility of an inflationary monetary policy being adopted supposedly because of a wage push, consider such an eventuality as a "criticism" of the monetary theory of inflation. For example, we read:

> Although the monetarists have performed a valuable service by their emphasis on the importance of the money supply, they have marred their case by their too exclusive emphasis on that factor....

> The monetarists can...object that increased wage demands will not lead to inflation unless the supply of active money is increased. If its supply is not increased and the wage demands are accepted...the penalty will be a lower level of employment and output. It may then be argued that, even if costs and prices rise in this way, such a rise cannot properly be described as inflation....The weakness of this line of argument is, of course, its neglect of the strong political forces that will come into play. For government is then presented with a harsh dilemma. Should it...incur the penalty of higher unemployment and loss of output? Or should it allow total monetary expenditure, public and private, to rise and thus incur the penalty of inflation?[25]

A few considerations can be opposed to the above argument. First, to say that inflation is the result of an expansionary monetary policy "made inevitable" by a wage push does not amount to a theory of inflation different from the monetary one. Even in the absence of a wage push an excessively expansionary monetary policy would result in inflation, and, without such a monetary growth, a wage push would not produce inflation. On the author's own admission, the monetary theory is thus confirmed.

Second, it is highly debatable to say that the best way to deal with irresponsible trade unions is that of imposing inflation on the whole economy so that the negative effects of their action can be mitigated. Footing the bill of extravagant demands of the unions does not recommend itself as the best way to restore responsibility in collective bargaining.

Third, to say that excessive wage increases confront the government with the dilemma of choosing between higher unemployment and a loss of output on the one hand, or higher inflation on the other[26] is the same as saying that one can trade a bit less unemployment for a bit more inflation. This idea, which is at the heart of the Phillips Curve, is now generally discredited, both on theoretical grounds and because of the experience of the last few years, which have been marked by both (higher) inflation and (higher) unemployment.[27]

The idea that one could offset the negative impact of the trade unions' excessive wage demands by deliberately implementing an inflationary monetary policy has had devastating effects on the economies of many Western countries. For it has encouraged (indeed rewarded) trade union irresponsibility, while injecting inflation into the economic system to the point that it is now endemic, and creating the conditions for a permanently higher rate of unemployment. In light of the experience of the last few years, monetarism is vindicated not only as a positive theory of inflation, but also as a normative policy prescription of how to deal with it.

This being said, it must be added that the non-automatic connection between "excessive" wage increases and an inflationary monetary policy aimed at accommodating them holds true *only for the private sector*, or for countries where the public sector is small relative to the private sector. As we shall see in the next chapter, the situation is quite different for those Western democracies where the public sector is excessively large. In such countries, the structure of incentives makes collective bargaining in the public sector biased in favor of excessive wage increases. These, in turn, result in the rapid increase of total public sector spending and, after the government deficit reaches a very high level, inevitably lead to the "financing" of the deficit through money creation. However, even in such a case, the true cause of the inflationary monetary policy is not the wage push *per se,* but the extravagant size of the public sector. The point deserves further illustration.

Supporters of the wage push doctrine rest their case on the assumption that wage increases have been "excessive," and blame labor unions for this. I find such a conclusion to be paradoxical: why blame those who *get* an excessive wage increase rather than those who *grant* it? If I get more than I should, that serves my interest. If a businessman pays labor services more than he should, he brings ruin upon

23

himself. What is puzzling, therefore, about excessive wage increases is not the behavior of those who get them, but rather the behavior of those who grant them. In other words, why blame the unions for the excessive increase in wages? The truth is that countries that suffer from excessive wage increases should hold statism responsible for them, not the unions. What happens is that managers of public firms willingly surrender "public" money to the unions in order to buy "social peace." The process is remarkably similar to that of trying to buy out an extortionist, with similar results.[28] The process provides further evidence in favor of the well-known axiom that inflation invariably has its roots in the government sector of the economy.

It is worth stressing again, however, that unless statism on a large scale and an unusually large government deficit combine in making money creation as the only way to pay for excessive wage increases in the public sector, there is no necessary, automatic connection between wage increases and an inflationary monetary policy. Under "normal" circumstances, an expansionary monetary policy is the wrong way to respond to trade union pressures, because it encourages their irresponsibility, makes inflation endemic or very hard to cure, and raises the long run unemployment rate. In any case, the wage push is not an autonomous explanation of inflation, which occurs if, and only if, the money supply grows faster than output.

Public Deficits

Another non-monetary theory is that which considers the government deficit as the cause of inflation. It must be stressed here that, as in the previous case of the wage push, government deficit is not an autonomous cause of inflation if it is financed by money creation. We need to distinguish the government deficit as a cause of inflation from the deficit as a cause of money creation. In this latter case we do not have a theory of inflation alternative to the monetary one — the government deficit is just one of the innumerable reasons behind an inflationary monetary policy. Let us consider the two cases separately, starting from a government deficit that does not lead to money creation.

It is clear from what we have said before that this would be the typical Keynesian case, were not the Keynesians reluctant to accept a demand-induced explanation of inflation for the reasons stated above. Indeed, as we have seen, the government deficit is the key policy variable in the Keynesian approach to demand management. Hence, any Keynesian version of the demand pull inflation would have to be based on the role of the government deficit.

The government deficit need not be financed by money creation.

Unless its size relative to national income grows beyond the government's capacity to borrow from the market, it can be financed by borrowing. The issue of government bonds to finance the deficit will not be without consequences on the economy. Presumably, the total supply of bonds will be increased, and this in turn will put an upward pressure on interest rates. As interest rates increase, some private productive investments will be discouraged (and saving stimulated). At the end of the process, the financing of the deficit will have reduced private spending—both investment and consumption—by an equal amount. This is usually referred to as "crowding out" private spending, and it has important consequences on the economy. In the words of Richard E. Wagner and Robert D. Tollison:

> Crowding out private borrowing will, in turn, bring about a reduction in our standard of living. This reduction can be prevented only if government borrowing replaces the private investment that was crowded out and if it is as efficient as the private investment. . . . While some government borrowing is for investment, most of it is for consumption. This means that budget deficits replace the creation of capital goods with the subsidization of consumption. By crowding out investment for consumption, deficit finance results in capital consumption.[29]

Capital consumption, in turn, results in a slower rate of growth of the economy and, possibly, in a higher rate of unemployment.

But, what about inflation? There is no reason to believe that the government deficit *per se* will increase spending relative to output, if the quantity of money is kept under control. And yet, some economists believe that, even if the deficit is entirely financed by borrowing from the market, it will result in inflation. Thus, Professor Minford has recently come out in favor of the view that "inflation is caused by budget deficits."[30] It is not clear whether he is convinced that inflation results from the mere existence of a government deficit, or if it is due to the fact that "monetary policy cannot be systematically independent of the budget deficit." However, if the budget deficit does not result in a faster rate of growth of the money supply relative to output, why should it cause inflation?

As Samuel Brittan has pointed out in the discussion on Professor Minford's paper, it is not clear why the issue of government bonds should be inflationary, whereas the issue of private bonds should not have such an effect. Professor Minford's answer that "the private sector issue of bonds is matched by a private sector acquisition of assets, so they cancel out," whereas the same is not true in the case of government bonds, is not entirely convincing. If inflation is determined by the level of spending relative to output, there is no reason why the *composition* of assets held by the public should give birth to a *sus-*

25

tained inflationary process. In order to continue spending in excess of output, people must be given more money to spend. If the quantity of money is kept constant, how are they going to finance their excess spending?

One possible answer to that problem is that the increase in interest rates produced by the issue of government bonds reduces the demand for money, i.e., it increases velocity, so that the price level may rise even if the quantity of money is fixed.[31] However, as we have seen, the decumulation of cash balances may finance a once-and-for-all increase in the price level, but, since cash balances are limited, it cannot finance a *sustained* inflationary process.

Supporters of the view that inflation is caused by the government deficit usually end up resorting to the alternative version of the impossibility to finance the deficit without money creation.[32] If such is the case, however, we are again in a monetarist world, inflation being caused by too rapid an increase in the quantity of money, and the government deficit being the reason for such an excessive monetary growth.

As we shall see in the next chapter, this is an accurate interpretation of events in countries where the ratio of the government deficit to national income is so high that it would be impossible for the government to borrow enough from the market to finance the deficit without resorting to money creation. However, this need not be the case in countries where the budget deficit is small relative to national income. For example, one sees little problem in borrowing from the public 1.5 or 2 percent of national income, which appears to be the ratio of the budget deficit to GNP for most of the industrialized countries of the West.[33] For such countries, the size of the government deficit becomes a scapegoat for an avoidable excessive growth of the money supply. They have no justification for not keeping the quantity of money under control and thereby putting an end to the inflationary process.

The "Oil Crisis"

Another non-monetary theory of inflation is that which blames it on external or "imported" factors. As we have seen, this is not a new explanation of the origin of inflation: it was very popular at the time of the German hyperinflation, when German writers blamed the cause of the process on reparation payments. The idea that inflation is imported from abroad, however, has received considerable attention in recent times because of the so-called "oil crisis." Many economic observers maintain that the "new" inflation of the 1970s has its origin in the increase in the price of imported oil due to the OPEC price cartel. It should be obvious from what we have said about the German inflation that the previous considerations can be applied here. Given the popularity of the notion, however, it might be worth devoting a few further comments to this problem.

We must stress once again that, if the idea that inflation has its roots in the increase in the price of imported oil wants to be an autonomous explanation of inflation, different from the monetary one, it must rest on a direct causal connection between the increase in the price of oil and inflation, rather than on an expansionary monetary policy "caused by" the oil price increase. In such a case, we would obviously be back into a monetary world, with the oil price increase being just another "justification" for an excessive rate of growth of the money supply. Let us, therefore, assume that the quantity of money is kept under control, and briefly analyze the effects of the increase in the price of imported oil.

If the demand for oil is inelastic relative to price — if the quantity demanded decreases relatively less than the percentage increase in price — the oil price increase will determine an increase in aggregate spending on oil. Assuming that all other expenditures remain unchanged, total aggregate spending will increase. How is such an increase going to be financed? If the quantity of money is kept under control, it will have to be financed by a decumulation of "idle" cash balances (an increase in velocity). As a result of such an increase in spending, the price level will increase (if real output does not increase in the same proportion at the same time). However, as we have seen, this does not allow us to talk of inflation, because a *sustained* inflationary process cannot be financed by a decumulation of cash balances. Since these are limited, the price level increase will have to come, sooner or later, to an end. If the quantity of money is kept under control, therefore, the "exogenous" increase in the price of oil cannot cause inflation.

Furthermore, the assumptions on which we have based our conclusion of a once-and-for-all increase in the price level due to the oil price increase are far from being unconditionally true. First, whether the price elasticity of demand for oil is less than one or not is something that must be assessed empirically. The numerical value of that elasticity cannot be assumed on an *a priori* basis. Even from an *a priori* perspective, however, while it is plausible to assume that the demand for oil is relatively inelastic with respect to price *for small price increases*, it is highly doubtful that the same is true for large increases. Second, a small increase in expenditures on oil might leave other expenditures unchanged and thus result in an increase in aggregate spending. But, if the increase in spending on oil is large relative to income, it will be likely to be financed (at least partially) by a decrease in other expenditures. Finally, there is no *a priori* reason that allows us to assume that the increase in spending must of necessity exceed the rate of real growth. Therefore, even the once-and-for-all increase in the price level due to the oil price rise rests on hypothetical assumptions. (Their plausibility does not "prove" anything.)

The effects of the oil price increase, however, are not limited to aggregate spending but concern other economic variables. If the country spends more on imported oil because of the price rise, this will result in a balance of payments deficit and, eventually, in a fall in the exchange rate. The problem is very similar to that of Germany's reparation payments mentioned before. If the quantity of money is prevented from rising, however, the fall in the exchange rate will tend to restore equilibrium in the balance of payments by stimulating exports and discouraging imports. In real terms, at the end of the process, the country will pay for its increased expenditure on oil imports by an increased export of goods and services. If, on the other end, the exchange rate is prevented from falling, balance of payments equilibrium will have to be achieved by domestic deflation: a decline in domestic incomes and prices will stimulate exports and discourage imports until equilibrium is restored at the existing exchange rate.

It is not unlikely that some deflationary pressures will result from the increased price of oil in any case. If the money supply fails to grow, the increase in the price of oil will translate itself into an autonomous increase in costs and, since aggregate spending remains unchanged, in lower employment and real income growth. How far this process will go depends, of course, on a number of circumstances, and cannot be assessed on *a priori* grounds.

It must be mentioned that the adjustment process briefly summarized above is not accepted by some economists who support the idea of a "vicious circle." Their argument is remarkably similar—if not identical—to that of the German writers. According to this view, the fall in the exchange rate will make imports more expensive in terms of the domestic currency. The increase in the price of imports will in turn result in an increase in cost for those industries that need imported raw materials. These will have to raise prices because of the increase in costs, and, since their products are often exported, the country's exports will become less competitive. Rather than eliminating the deficit, the fall in the exchange rate will result, according to this view, in an increased balance of payments deficit on the one end, and in "imported" inflation on the other. It must be noted at this point that, as for the adjustment problem, if this view is correct, the solution is quite simple. What these writers are saying is that a fall in the exchange rate will eventually result in an increased deficit. But, if this is the case, all that is needed is an *increase* in the rate: this would presumably result in a decrease in the domestic price of imports and an increased competitiveness of exports.[34]

The decisive argument against the "vicious circle" hypothesis is that it implicitly assumes — on *a priori* grounds — that, regardless of what happens to monetary policy, there cannot be an equilibrium value of the exchange rate. No matter how much the exchange rate falls, that is, the balance of payments will always be in deficit, regardless of the internal rate of inflation. Such an assumption is amply refuted by the evidence and is absolutely unacceptable.

As for the effect of the "oil crisis" on domestic inflation, the situation has been very clearly summarized by Professor Haberler:

> It is understandable that the authorities everywhere try to put the blame for the inflation on the rise of oil prices. But that the root of inflation lies elsewhere, namely in monetary and financial policies, is demonstrated by the fact that in recent years the United States had persistently a much higher inflation rate than the strong-currency countries — Germany, Japan, Switzerland, and some others — although those countries rely on imported oil to a much greater extent than the United States. The fact that Canada, an energy-rich country, had even more inflation than the United States is further proof that the oil price rise is not the dominant cause of world inflation.[35]

And, as for the size of the problem:

> The *Economic Report of the President* (1980) puts the U.S. share in the increased oil bill at almost $45 billion. This is a large sum, but in a $2.5 trillion economy it cannot be called a crushing burden. It is less than 2 percent of the gross national product and less than one-half of what might be called the normal annual growth of GNP. (. . .)I repeat, the oil price rise is not a crushing burden for the United States, and the same is true of the other industrial countries and the more advanced among the less developed countries.[36]

In the light of the available evidence, it is probably not unfair to maintain that the idea that the "new" inflation must be blamed on the oil price rise is just the latest in the long history of scapegoats for a problem that is of our own making, that does not fall on us from the outside, but is created by the domestic monetary and fiscal policies of the country.[37] And what has been said about the oil crisis can be extended to the idea that inflation can be "imported" via a balance of payments surplus. In such a case, inflation is not "imported" but it is due to the Central Bank's commitment to a fixed exchange rate coupled with its inability to offset the inflow of liquidity.

Productivity and Inflation

Before we leave the non-monetary explanations of inflation, mention must be made of the view of those who blame inflation on sluggish productivity. The idea is that, if the rate of real income growth were higher, the rate of inflation, for a given rate of growth of aggregate spending, would be lower. The culprits in this line of reasoning are, once again, the trade unions, accused of slowing down the rate of growth of the economy and of diminishing the productive efficiency of the country. Now, it is obvious that the standard of living of the country, in real terms, and its improvement over time, crucially depend on productivity. Nothing is more important than productivity in determining how well-off people are in terms of real income. However, from the point of view of inflation, productivity is not as important, for a very simple reason. In the words of Milton Friedman:

> As a matter of theory, a one percentage point increase in productivity will reduce inflation rates by one percentage point a year just as much as a one percentage point reduction in the rate of monetary growth. But the range within which productivity can vary...is very narrow. One or two percentage points difference is very important. On the other hand, as you all know from experience, the range over which monetary growth can vary is enormous. You can go...from a negative rate of growth in one quarter to a rate of growth of 24% a year two quarters later. And consequently as a practical matter, the variations in the rate of monetary growth absolutely swamp any effect of variations in productivity. Hence, for the purpose of controlling inflation, productivity is not a major matter.[38]

The few remarks made so far do not cover more than a very narrow fraction of the non-monetary explanations of inflation. For our present purposes, however, they should be adequate to show that, in most cases, the non-monetary explanations do not really amount to alternative theories. What these explanations seek to analyze is the reason(s) behind the excessive growth of the money supply, but they do not contradict the view that the only proximate cause of inflation is the rapid rate of monetary growth. If the quantity of money, for whatever reason, grows faster than output, inflation will result, and no sustained inflationary process is possible without an excessive rate of monetary growth. Monetary policy, therefore, is both the necessary and sufficient condition for inflation to occur.

This being said, however, there still remains the problem of ascertaining the reasons behind the adoption of inflationary monetary policies. Money, as we have said, is only the proximate cause of inflation. The rapid growth in the quantity of money itself might be the consequence of something else.

Government and Inflation

Lenin was certainly right. There is no subtler, no surer means of overturning the existing basis of Society than to debauch the currency. The process engages all the hidden forces of economic law on the side of destruction, and does it in a manner which not one man in a million is able to diagnose.

John Maynard Keynes, 1919

Inflation has accelerated throughout the world, and it must be particularly disturbing to Keynesian policy-makers that the countries where their influence was greatest are those which have suffered most....So how is it, a sensible Keynesian might ask, that the countries where those in power and influence have the most correct understanding of how economies work managed to achieve the worst results and to be among the world's perpetual candidates for international financial support?

Walter Eltis, 1976

Inflation is Not The Rule

Inflation is not the normal state of affairs. If we look at the various indices of the cost of living, we see that in many cases monetary stability has been the rule, rather than the exception. This is true even for countries that are currently plagued by very high rates of inflation. In what follows we shall explicitly examine the case of Italy. It is worth, therefore, to start by looking at the inflationary history of that country.

In contrast with her long cultural history, Italy is a relatively young country: her birth as a unified nation can be set at the time of the proclamation of the Kingdom of Italy in 1861. During these 120 years, Italy has experienced a wide variety of political changes: a monarchy for 85 years, and a republic since 1946; a limited ("elite") democracy from 1861 to 1915, a dictatorship from 1922 to World War II, an unlimited ("mass") democracy from 1946 to the present. Despite all these major changes in the political arrangements of the country, the peacetime history of Italy is one of great monetary stability — with the exception of the last decade.

In Table 1, the average annual rate of change in the cost of living in-

Table 1
Italy: Average Annual Rate of Inflation.

1861	–	1870	+	0.29	
1870	–	1880	+	1.59	
1880	–	1890	–	0.53	
1890	–	1900	–	0.48	
1900	–	1910	+	0.85	
1910	–	1914	+	1.27	
1915	–	1922			(see Table 2)
1922	–	1935	–	1.43	
1935	–	1939	+	6.10	
1940	–	1950			(see Table 2)
1950	–	1960	+	3.04	
1960	–	1970	+	4.21	
1970	–	1980	+	13.55	

dex is presented. Data show that from the time of the proclamation of the Kingdom of Italy to World War I, prices were stable: changes in the cost of living index were minor and took place in both directions. It was a period of zero inflation, with only modest fluctuations in the price level. In 1915, at the time of Italy's entry into World War I, the cost of living index was only 21 percent above its 1861 level. It had taken 54 years to arrive at an increase that is not uncommon to achieve in one year in our inflationary times.

World War I was a period of unprecedented inflation (Table 2). However, the inflationary episode had very limited duration, judged from today's standards. Even if one, somewhat arbitrarily, includes the two post-war years of high inflation, the whole inflationary period is limited to six years: by 1922, prices had actually started to decline.

From 1922 to 1935, Italy experienced a period of moderate (even if prolonged) deflation: prices were declining at the rate of 1.4 percent

Table 2

1915	+	7.00	1940	+	16.69	1970	+	5.08
1916	+	25.14	1941	+	15.70	1971	+	4.80
1917	+	41.44	1942	+	15.58	1972	+	5.72
1918	+	39.44	1943	+	67.70	1973	+	10.83
1919	+	1.51	1944	+	344.40	1974	+	19.13
1920	+	31.40	1945	+	96.95	1975	+	16.95
1921	+	18.30	1946	+	18.01	1976	+	16.77
1922	–	0.60	1947	+	62.06	1977	+	18.36
			1948	+	5.87	1978	+	13.23
			1949	+	1.46	1979	+	18.22
			1950	–	1.34	1980	+	19.98

Based on the Cost of Living Index. *See Indici dei prezzi al consumo per le famiglie di operai ed impiegati (gia' indici del costo della vita), 1861–1978,* Istituto Centrale di Statistica, Roma, 1979, anno III, n. 2.

per year. If we set the cost of living index of 1922 equal to 100, in 1935 it was 82.7: a decline of 17.3 percent in 14 years. The last year of Fascism, before World War II, were marked by "trotting" inflation: from 1935 to 1939, prices were rising at the rate of 6 percent per year. Then the great inflation of World War II started; an unprecedented episode in terms of duration, and still unequaled in terms of magnitude. The great inflation of World War II was terminated by the end of 1948. It is worth mentioning that the return of monetary stability was achieved by the "orthodox" monetary measures of Luigi Einaudi—a free market economist and a firm believer in the importance of price stability. His "monetarist" policies set Italy on a growth path: the 1950s were a period of rapid economic development, the time of the so-called "Italian economic miracle."

The 1950s, however, were also a period of "creeping" inflation: prices were rising at an average rate of 3 percent per year, and this was generally interpreted as evidence that some degree of inflation was the unavoidable cost of rapid growth. At the beginning of the 1960s, the move to the "center-left"—the socialist-oriented coalition government—meant a change in economic philosophy: price stability was no longer regarded as a primary goal of economic policy.

As a result of this change in perspective, the first half of the 1960s experienced relatively high rates of inflation. The peak was reached in 1963, when inflation exceeded 7.5 percent. Despite the drastic drop in the inflation rate in the second half of the 1960s, the overall rate for the decade is still higher than that of the previous decade: 4.2 percent. These first 110 years of Italian monetary history can be summarized by saying that, with the exception of the two World Wars, inflation had been moderate or absent—never reaching a double digit level, and almost always below 5 percent per year. Furthermore, the whole period before 1935—with the aforementioned exception of World War I—has been a period of price stability, with only moderate rates of inflation or deflation.

In marked contrast with this whole period, the inflation rate in the last decade has been significantly above the 10 percent mark. It is an inflationary episode that has no precedent in the peacetime history of the country. The so-called "new" inflation of the 1970s can be compared—in terms of duration, if not of magnitude—with that of the two World Wars. From this point of view, the phenomenon is indeed new and it is, therefore, worth trying to analyze its roots.

Money and Inflation in the 1970s

It is a known fact in monetary theory that there is a time lag between a change in monetary growth and the resulting effect on inflation. From this perspective, Keynes' famous statement that "in the long run, we are all dead" is absolutely wrong. The truth is that we always live in the long run, in the sense that what happens today is almost always the consequence of past events. Today's inflation rate is the result of the rate of monetary growth of several months ago, not of today's. In a sense, therefore, today is the last day of a long run initiated sometime in the past.

The measurement of the time lag in the reaction of output and prices to monetary changes is one of the more difficult problems in monetary analysis. What makes it particularly difficult is the fact that there is no fixed, stable time interval that is valid for all countries and for all times. The reaction to a change in monetary growth rates may take a few weeks or several months, depending on the institutional framework of the country, the state of inflationary expectations, etc. In some countries, the time interval between a change in monetary growth and the resulting effect on the inflation rate is two years.

For the US, the UK, and Japan, the lag between a change in monetary growth and output is roughly six to nine months, between the change in monetary growth and inflation, roughly two years. Of course, the effects are spread out, not concentrated at the indicated point of time.[1]

Furthermore, as should be obvious given the definition of inflation, the rate of inflation is not necessarily equal — after a time lag — to the rate of growth of the money supply, because changes in output (and, possibly, also in velocity) must be taken into account.

The striking peculiarity of the "new" inflation in Italy in the 1970s is that the behavior of the inflation rate conforms to the predictions of the quantity theory of money in its most simplified, crude version, with a two year lag. In other words, even if one disregards changes in output and ignores the problem of the "spreading out" of the effects of monetary growth, the rate of inflation over time mirrors monetary changes with a fixed two year lag for the whole decade. (see Table 3)[2]

These figures should suggest that what is "new" about the inflation in Italy in the 1970s is not its origin — which is strikingly monetary in nature — but its size and duration, which are unprecedented in the peacetime history of the country. As for the opinion of those who regard the change in the money supply as the consequence of inflation, rather than its cause, it obviously does not hold in this case (it never does): inflation could not possibly *cause* the monetary change that had taken place two years earlier.

If the Italian inflation of the 1970s provides further evidence in support of the monetary theory of inflation, the question then becomes that of ascertaining *why* the quantity of money has grown more ra-

Table 3

Money (M_1) 1970–1978 = 100		Consumer Price Index 1972–1980 = 100	
1970	47.3	51.1	1972
1971	56.3	56.6	1973
1972	66.0	67.4	1974
1973	82.0	78.9	1975
1974	89.7	92.1	1976
1975	101.8	109.0	1977
1976	121.0	123.4	1978
1977	149.4	146.0	1979
1978	186.0	175.1	1980*

Based on Banca d'Italia data for M_1, and ISTAT figures for the Consumer Price Index. The figure for 1980* is an estimate. M_1 = Currency + Demand Deposits, end of the year.

pidly than output. The Italian experience confirms Fritz Machlup's point of view:

> The creation of highpowered money is not a mechanical, automatic process, but the result of deliberate decisions and actions by the monetary authorities. (p. 300)

> In the course of the last three centuries the worst money-and-price inflations have been artless budget inflations. Government expenditures ran far above tax revenues, and the deficit could be covered only by printing paper money or borrowing newly created bank money. The governments had no special ideas or designs regarding the consequences; they simply could not help spending but could not get enough money from taxing the people or from borrowing funds which the people had saved from their current incomes. These "artless" budget deficits have occurred in the past chiefly to finance defense and war expenditures when a government found it impossible, for political reasons, to raise enough taxes to meet expenses. (p. 294)[3]

Deficits and Money Creation

If the interpretation of the above figures is correct, it suggests that the "new" inflation in Italy in the 1970s, which is still going on and whose end is not in sight, is a monetary phenomenon, produced by a more rapid growth in the quantity of money than in output. The question then becomes: why did the quantity of money grow so fast? In other words, if, as Machlup says, the "creation of highpowered money is...the result of deliberate decisions and actions by the monetary authorities", why did the Central Bank make the money supply grow to the point of producing such an unprecedented inflation?

The answer to this question is often very difficult. But, in the case of Italy, it seems to me that the explanation is fairly obvious. In order to understand why monetary policy in Italy has been so highly inflationary, one needs to look at the size of the government deficit, both in absolute terms and in relation to the country's income, and to its growth over time. The picture that emerges is, in terms of the magnitude of the deficit, very different from that of other countries, even of those, such as Great Britain, that are experiencing similar problems.

In Table 4 the absolute value of the government deficit in nominal terms from 1960 on is compared to Italy's gross domestic product in order to arrive at the ratio of the public deficit to national income — which, by the way, is one of the indicators of the financial irresponsibility of the government.

Table 4

	Government Deficit*	Gross Domestic Product Market Prices**	Government Deficit/GDP (%)
	(billions of lire)	(billions of lire)	
1960	− 382	21,632	1.8
1961	− 357	24,118	1.5
1962	− 570	27,117	2.1
1963	− 768	31,053	2.5
1964	− 817	33,941	2.4
1965	− 1,545	36,530	4.2
1966	− 1,823	39,521	4.6
1967	− 1,226	43,517	2.8
1968	− 2,022	46,953	4.3
1969	− 1,692	51,691	3.3
1970	− 3,226	57,937	5.6
1971	− 4,759	63,056	7.5
1972	− 5,745	69,080	8.3
1973	− 7,972	89,746	8.9
1974	− 8,961	110,719	8.1
1975	− 16,523	125,378	13.2
1976	− 14,707	156,657	9.4
1977	− 22,531	190,083	11.9
1978	− 34,090	222,254	15.3
1979	− 30,075	269,657	11.2
1980	− 39,200	337,402	11.6

*Source: International Monetary Fund, *International Financial Statistics*, 1979, and February 1981.
**Sources: Istituto Centrale di Statistica, *Le Regioni in Cifre*, Roma, 1979; Istituto Centrale di Statistica, *I Conti degli Italiani*, Roma, 1979; International Monetary Fund, *International Financial Statistics*, op. cit. The figures from 1975 on refer to the "new" series, following the 1979 upward revision. For such a revision, see Franco Reviglio, *Il significato economico della rivalutazione dei conti nazionali*, unpublished paper, ISPE, June 1979.

In order to understand the time pattern of the deficit, one must keep in mind that a change in the government coalition took place at the beginning of the 1960s. The Italian Socialist Party (PSI) replaced the Italian Liberal Party (PLI). That change meant much less emphasis on monetary stability and an ideological preference for government growth. This pattern can easily be seen in both the absolute and the relative size of the government deficit from 1962 on.

In 1961, at the end of the "liberal" era, the government deficit was 357 billion lire, or 1.5 percent of GDP. By 1965 it had increased to 1,545 billion lire: 4.2 percent of GDP; in 1970 it had reached 3,226 billion, 5.6 percent of GDP. Then, the explosion of the 1970s followed: from the 3,226 billion lire of 1970 the deficit climbed to the 39,200 billion lire of 1980: from 5.6 percent to almost 12 percent. It is worth stressing that the *absolute* value of the government deficit in Italy is comparable to that of the United States: at the then going exchange rate, the 39,200 billion lire of the 1980 deficit equalled $44 billion. Obviously, in terms of financial irresponsibility, Italy is an economic giant, on a par with the United States.

What is even more extraordinary is that, in relative terms, the Italian government deficit far surpasses that of even the United Kingdom, which is another notorious example of the wonderful effects of an economic policy of "deficit spending." From 1971 to 1979 the ratio of the Public Sector Borrowing Requirement (the gracious label the English attach to their government deficit) to GNP in Great Britain has averaged slightly more than 6 percent, which is almost exactly one half the comparable ratio in Italy.[4]

Let's now look at the time pattern of the rate of growth of the quantity of money in comparison with the time pattern of the government deficit. In Table 5, the average value of the ratio of the government deficit to GNP is compared to the average value of the annual rate of growth of the quantity of money (M_1) in the quinquennia from 1960 to 1980.

The figures in Table 5 suggest that the rate of monetary growth in Italy has increased with the size of the ratio of the deficit to national

Table 5

			Government Deficit/GDP (%), Average	Average annual rate of growth of M1 (%)
1960	–	1964	2.06	13.69
1965	–	1969	3.84	14.65
1970	–	1974	7.68	19.47
1975	–	1979	12.20	20.73
1980*			11.60	22.00

M_1 = Currency + Demand Deposits, end of the year; source: Banca d'Italia.

income: from the average annual rate of 13 percent in 1960–1964, the rate of monetary growth has increased to an average of more than 20 percent in 1975–1979, *pari passu* with the relative size of the deficit.

The government's financial irresponsibilty as illustrated by the above figures has had devastating effects on the real productive capacity of the country. Before we go on to examine the reasons that have made recourse to money creation as a way to finance the deficit inevitable, let's briefly mention that massive borrowing has accompanied the explosion in the deficit. Public debt has risen from 22,665 billion lire in 1970 to 168,395 billion lire in 1979. In the words of the Governor of the Bank of Italy: "the ratio of public debt to GNP has reached 70% at the end of 1978; it was roughly 45% in 1968–70."[5]

What this has meant is that the need to finance the government deficit through borrowing has resulted in the massive destruction of credit and in the crowding out of private productive investments. The destruction of new credit by public borrowing has averaged 58.5 percent per year from 1973 to 1978.[6] The effect of this on productivity, employment, and growth needs no comment.

And yet, together with such a massive amount of borrowing from the market, the government deficit has also resulted, as the figures in Table 5 show, in very rapid monetary growth. We must now turn to examine the reasons behind this.

Monetary Growth Inevitable?

The possible explanations of the monetary financing of the government deficit are several and they are not mutually incompatible.

a) The first reason might be the desire to avoid excessive pressures on interest rates that might result from the attempt to finance the deficit entirely through recourse to the market. Such is, for example, the opinion of T. D. Willett and L. O. Laney: "It is usually the concern over limiting interest rate increases that leads monetary authorities to finance budget deficits through money creation."[7]

This might very well be true, but it is far from clear that the monetary financing of the deficit will result in lower interest rates in the long run. As Milton Friedman has pointed out:

> Over any long period of time the answer is clear. High monetary growth means high inflation, and high inflation produces high interest rates. Low monetary growth means low inflation, and low inflation produces low interest rates.
>
> Over shorter periods, the situation is more complex. The initial impact of slower monetary growth is to raise interest rates; of faster monetary growth, to lower interest rates.[8]

The fact that the attempt to keep interest rates down through an expansionary monetary policy is going to be frustrated in the long run, however, does not necessarily mean that monetary authorities are going to abstain from it. Even though they might be aware of the fact that monetary financing of the budget will, in the long run, result in *higher* (rather than lower) interest rates might be of little significance for them, if their time horizon is limited to the short run. This might very well be the case in a country, such as Italy, where frequent government crises make the "political cycle" as short as a few months. In such a climate of political instability the temptation to limit one's concern to the immediate future, leaving the long run negative consequences of one's decisions to the following administration, is unusually strong.

Even though the decision to try to keep interest rates down by means of monetary expansion is not wise from a long run perspective I would not rule out the possibility that the Italian monetary authorities have, consciously or unconsciously, been influenced by that consideration.

b) The second reason that might induce the monetary authorities to choose to finance the government deficit through money creation has to do with the system of political incentives. This has been well summarized by R. E. Wagner and R. D. Tollison:

> There is no mechanical connection between budget deficits and the stock of money, but this does not imply the absence of an actual connection between budget deficits and money creation.

But, why should the monetary authorities *choose* to finance the deficit through "debt monetization," i.e. money creation? According to the authors, the answer is quite simple:

> The political gains from deficit finance vary in direct proportion to the degree of diffusion of the costs of budget deficits among the population. A cost of $10 billion spread over one hundred million people will generally provoke less opposition than the same cost spread over only one million people. To the extent that budget deficits are financed by genuine government borrowing, the costs of deficit finance will be concentrated upon the investors who are crowded out. In contrast, money creation will diffuse the cost among the population. Therefore, since deficit finance accompanied by money creation will diffuse the cost more generally, it will evoke less opposition than deficit finance in the absence of money creation.[9]

The idea that monetary authorities might choose to finance the government deficit through money creation because, by so doing, they reduce the amount of opposition to deficit finance, is a variation on a well-known theme. The fact is that inflation is a tax on nominal assets that does not need any formal procedure of legislation to be enacted and is not perceived by those who "pay" it as a tax. Therefore, inflation is a very convenient way to finance government spending ("convenient" for the government, that is). Government can increase spending without having to go through the complicated and unpopular procedure of introducing new taxes, and the people will pay the hidden tax of inflation without knowing that it is a tax. Most people will not even be aware of its nature and its origin, and will blame it on a variety of scapegoats — from Arab sheiks to trade unions. There is, therefore, a strong presumption that the structure of political incentives will make inflationary finance politically palatable. In a country where the Central Bank is as conditioned by political incentives as the government itself, debt monetization will be a probable outcome.

This being said, it is hard to know on *a priori* grounds what role this factor has played in the rapid rate of monetary growth in Italy. It would be extremely hard to provide evidence in support of such a conjecture, even if one assumes that it is possible to test it (which is doubtful).

Let me stress that what we are concerned with here are not the pressures in favor of a larger government deficit. These exist and have undoubtedly played a major role in the explosion of the government deficit in Italy. Our problem now is: given the size of the deficit, why should an independent Central Bank deliberately *choose* to finance it through money creation? To say that money creation will diffuse the cost of the deficit finance among the population and, therefore, prove to be a more palatable strategy, completely ignores the fact that central bankers are not elected officials and that they often derive genuine pride from their success in guaranteeing monetary stability. In order for that hypothesis to hold in a country, such as Italy, where the Central Bank is, at least nominally, independent, one would also have to assume that central bankers have given up their independence and become subservient to government pressures. This is not entirely unlikely, but it would very difficult to prove it.

The answer to this problem crucially depends on the size of the government deficit relative to national income. Granted that there are strong political pressures favoring increased government spending and opposing increased taxation, which we will examine in what follows, the resulting increased deficit needs not be financed by money creation unless its size exceeds a certain critical level. Thus, even in Great Britain, contrary to Professor Minford's previously quoted view, no clear connection between the size of the budget deficit and money creation has been established.

On the other hand, Professor Friedman maintains:

> Higher government spending provokes taxpayer resistance. Taxpayer resistance encourages government to finance spending by monetary creation, thereby increasing monetary growth and hence inflation, which,

as a by-product very welcome to legislators, raises effective tax rates without legislation.[10]

Professor Friedman's view is probably based on the further, implicit assumption that central bankers are not independent from the government and they are, therefore, likely to do whatever suits the interests of the government. If this is not so, however, taxpayer resistance, while a condition for increased government deficits, is not a sufficient condition for monetary creation. Unless the deficit exceeds a given percentage of national income, there is no reason why it *could* not be financed by genuine borrowing from the market. This, obviously, does not mean that monetary creation is not a widely used means of financing the deficit – it most definitely is – but there is no reason why this should inevitably be the case.

What can and does happen is that monetary authorities, in order to try to avoid a short-run increase in interest rates, or because they are concerned about the recessionary impact of the deficit, or because they are subject to the structure of political incentives and favor the diffusion of the cost of deficit financing achieved through money creation, or for a variety of other reasons, find it "convenient" to resort to debt monetization.

c) The problem of financing the government deficit crucially depends on its size. It is entirely possible to borrow from the market, for example 4.5 percent of gross domestic product – the ratio of the PSBR to GDP in the United Kingdom in 1979. If the Bank of England failed to do so, it was because other considerations played a role in making it pay for the deficit by creating money. But it could have chosen a different alternative. When, on the other hand, the ratio of the government deficit to national income totals 12 percent – as it did in Italy in 1980 – it is doubtful, if not impossible, that the Central Bank could have borrowed that much from the market.[11]

As long as the deficit remains small relative to national income, the Central Bank can choose whether to finance it through money creation or not. But, once it has reached a very high dimension, there is no alternative option: it can only be financed by printing money. This is true of war-time inflations, and it is also true of the "new" inflation in Italy in the 1970s. Finally, if the tendency toward greater and greater government deficits continues, other countries might end up in the same situation as Italy, with no alternative to an inflationary monetary policy as the only way to finance the deficit.

The Government Push

It would be very hard to set an exact figure for the critical value of the deficit beyond which debt monetization becomes inevitable. That figure obviously depends on many factors, such as the country's propensity to save, the private demand for credit, etc. Also, it really makes little difference to know whether the Central Bank *could* have avoided the financing of the deficit through money creation or not, as long as it does so. The crucial problem is a very different one, and to this we now turn.

If the above analysis is correct, inflation is a monetary phenomenon, produced by too rapid an increase in the quantity of money. In terms of the demand pull *vs.* cost push controversy, inflation must be seen as caused by excess demand. Such demand pull has its origin not in a cost push that has given rise to an inflationary monetary policy but to a *government push* that has resulted in the excessively rapid growth of the quantity of money. The situation has been very clearly summarized by Michael Parkin:

> ...[t]he attempt by vote-seeking governments to spend too big a fraction of national income either directly on goods and services or indirectly on social security benefits, and their unwillingness at the same time to levy taxes on a sufficient scale to cover that expenditure, leads to an excessive public sector borrowing requirement. Again with an eye on the electoral consequences, an unwillingness to see interest rates rise to sufficiently high levels ensures that, to a large extent, the public sector borrowing requirements is met by printing money.[12]

For a country such as Italy, where the government deficit is endemic (there has never been a surplus since World War II) and amounts to a substantial percentage of national income, excessively rapid monetary growth is the expected result of the *government push*. The deficit, in other words, is simply another indicator of the growth of government.

A good illustration of the growth of government in Italy is given by the ratio of public sector spending to national income. According to one estimate, this ratio—which measures the cost of government to the average Italian—has risen from 37 percent in 1960 to 44 percent in 1970. Official estimates indicate that the ratio has further increased from 49.2 percent in 1976 to 55.8 percent in 1979.[13] The estimate for public sector spending for 1980 set it at 163,102 billion lire ($192 billion, at the then current exchange rate): $3,400 for every Italian man and woman, rich or poor, young or old; $13,600, *on average*, for a family of four in one single year.[14]

It might be worth adding that the general feelings about the benefits of such a colossal amount of government spending are not exactly optimistic, if the then Minister of Finance ventured to suggest that as much as 40 percent of it might be devoted to pure waste.[15]

The tremendous growth in the size of government as measured by the ratio of public spending to national income, and the resulting explosion in the size of the deficit, have made monetary folly inevitable.

The annual rate of growth of the quantity of money (M_2), which reached the 25 percent mark in the second half of 1975, has remained consistently within the 20–25 percent range since then. When money grows at the annual rate of 25 percent, when the quantity of money doubles every 3–3½ years, it is little wonder that prices aren't stable. Not surprisingly, the purchasing power of the lira in 1980 was slightly more than one fourth its 1970 value. In the light of such a deterioration in the value of the monetary unit, few people would consider it an achievement that Italy is possibly the only country in the world where everybody is a millionaire (one million lire was worth slightly more than $1,100 dollars at the 1980 exchange rate.)

If the rapid growth in the quantity of money finds its origin in the government push, it might be worth investigating why the government has grown so rapidly. What follows represents only a brief summary of some of the factors that account for the growth of government. A detailed analysis, that would take into account the extensive recent work on the subject, would clearly exceed our present purpose.[16]

The Culprits

Only government can print money and, if inflation is the result of too rapid an increase in the quantity of money, only government can be the cause of inflation. (Counterfeiters also print money, but in most countries their contribution to the total quantity of money is absolutely negligible). However, unless one is prepared to accept some kind of "conspiracy theory" of society[17], we still need an explanation of the factors that account for the growth of government — the *government push*.

The growth of government is the unintended result of the working of some kind of perverse "invisible hand" operating in the political arena. Whereas the invisible hand in the *economic* market results in a socially beneficial outcome unintentionally achieved by the interaction of the behavior of the numerous market participants, all motivated by their self-interest, the invisible hand in the *political* market results in a socially deleterious outcome unintentionally produced by the interplay of the actions of the participants in the political game. In other words, whereas private and public interests go together in the economic market — in the sense that the interest of society is often served by the action of individuals pursuing their own private gain — in the political market they are often conflicting — in the sense that the pursuit of private gains by the various participants results not in a socially beneficial outcome but in a consequence that is detrimental to society. The irony of it is that many people, after having observed the evil effects of the invisible hand in the political market, instead of trying to devise solutions that would allow for its replacement with economic invisible hand devices, often end up recommending the "visible fist" of political coercion as an alternative.

Unless an appropriate fiscal constitution is adopted and enforced, the working of the political process under conditions of unlimited democracy inevitably results in excessive government growth. The excessive growth of government and its accompanying huge deficits inescapably produce increasing monetary instability that in due time plants the seeds of the destruction of democracy itself. In order to show how this undesirable outcome is brought about one needs to look at the structure of incentives for the various participants in the political process. We shall begin by looking at the sovereign of modern democracies: the voter.

The Voter

It is a common feature of many analyses of the problems of contemporary unlimited democracies that they tend to focus on the mistakes of the existing government. Most people tend to blame those who are currently in power for the perverse effects of the political process. Although there is much that can be said about the poor quality of our rulers, such an approach often neglects the main feature of democracy: politicians respond to pressures coming from their electorate. It is obviously tempting for a believer in the democratic system to put the blame of its malfunctions on inept or corrupt politicians. However, such a procedure does not absolve the system: if they are inept and corrupt, why were they elected? Furthermore, in most cases, the malfunctions of the political process find their origin in the voters' mandate that those who are in power cannot, and shoud not, ignore.

Since we are concerned with the growth of government, let us start by showing how this is to a large extent due to the structure of incentives for the voter. In order to do so, we can make use of a parable due to David Friedman:

> Special interest politics is a simple game. A hundred people sit in a circle, each with his pocket full of pennies. A politician walks around the outside of the circle, taking a penny from each person. No one minds; who cares about a penny? When he has gotten all the way around the circle, the politician throws fifty cents down in front of one person, who is overjoyed at the unexpected windfall. The process is repeated, ending with a different person. After a hundred rounds, everyone is a hundred cents poorer, fifty cents richer, and happy.[18]

This simple parable illustrates the main features of government intervention and explains how government growth is often brought

44

about by the requests of the voters. Let us look at these in turn.

First of all, the fact that at the end of the game the players receive less than they have paid stresses the distinguishing feature of statism, which I would call "public dissipation". I am not referring to the misallocation of resources created by government intervention, nor to the kind of waste that is usually associated with corruption. What I maintain now is that statism is of necessity a negative-sum game, in the sense that what society receives from the government is always and inevitably less than what society has been coerced to give to the government. The reason is quite simple: government intervention operates by imposing costs on some groups in society in order to hand out benefits to other groups. (Or taxing the whole of society in order to give to everybody). But, since the costs of transferring these resources are positive and increasing, the value of the benefits of government intervention is inevitably lower than the cost of government. And the difference grows with the growth of government. The most obvious example of these costs is given by bureaucratic costs.[19]

The second point illustrated by the parable is that, as long as government intervention is limited, even though the cost of government to society exceeds the benefit, some individuals or groups might gain from government intervention. But, when the government grows to very large dimensions, each individual ends up paying more than he is getting. Obviously, this is an exaggeration: even in an unlimited government system — such as that of communist countries — some individuals always gain from government intervention (i.e., the members of the ruling oligarchy). What is true is that, as government intervention increases, its cost falls on a larger and larger number of citizens. The state taxes everybody (including the poor) to give to everybody (including the rich). The result is that the number of people who lose because of government intervention increases. Statism also results in regressive redistribution: the government taxes (also) the poor in order to give (also) to the rich.

The parable also illustrates the bias in the incentive structure that leads to the growth of government. The situation is even more extreme in the real world. One billion dollars of government spending provides those who benefit from it with an incentive to promote its enactment that is roughly equal to $1 billion. (It is actually smaller than $1 billion, because, as we have just said, the benefit of a given government project is always smaller than its cost. However, if we include the bureaucrats employed in the project among the beneficiaries of it, then the *whole* group has a $1 billion incentive to make sure the project is enacted.) They will devote time and energy, putting pressure on politicians, lobbying, advertising the alleged benefits of the scheme on the media, etc., so that the desired spending project takes place. On the other hand, a $1 billion project, if its cost is evenly distributed among the whole population, would only cost $4.43 on average to each of the 226 million Americans. Each citizen, therefore, has only a $4.43 incentive to try to resist the enactment of that particular piece of legislation. Furthermore, the campaign in favor of the scheme will discourage those who do not benefit from it and must bear its cost from any active resistance to its implementation. For an amount equal, on average, only to $4.43 it is not worth risking to be accused of lacking compassion and sensitivity to "social" problems. ("Social" problems are usually those that can only be solved by spending someone else's money!)

As a result of this simple arithmetical asymmetry in incentives, pressures favoring the growth of government are necessarily stronger than pressures opposing it. Most people, rather than opposing projects that benefit others while costing them money, prefer to spend their time lobbying for projects that directly benefit themselves. As the size of the game grows, so does the size of government spending and the loss to society as a whole.

The problem is made more acute by the fact that the benefits of government action are concentrated and visible, whereas the cost of government intervention is usually dispersed among a large number of individuals and almost invisible. Very few people indeed are aware of how much of the cost of a given government project falls on them, whereas those who benefit from government spending are well aware of how much they stand to gain from its enactment. This difference in perception of the costs of government as compared to its benefits further strengthens the bias in the structure of incentives in favor of government growth.

But, it might be argued, if in the end everybody stands to lose from government growth, how is it that, as soon as people begin to understand how much government growth is costing them, they do not become actively involved in trying to tame it down? First of all, it is quite obvious from recent episodes both in Europe and in the United States that this kind of awareness on the part of public opinion is already present and quite visible. One needs only to remember Proposition 13 in California and similar referenda in other states, or the electoral results in a number of countries — from Great Britain, to Jamaica, to the United States — which clearly show a widespread desire for a reduction in the size of government. However, there is also a reason related to the structure of incentives that explains why these forces are likely to be defeated in their attempt to tame government. The reason is symmetrical to the above argument: a given reduction in government spending inflicts a damage on those who benefit from it that is greater than the benefit it confers on each of the other individuals in society. A reduction of government spending of $1 billion costs $1 billion to

46

those who are on the receiving end of the government project while the benefit of the reduction for the average American is only equal to $4.43. Therefore, pressures opposing the reduction in spending are likely to be much stronger and more effective than those favoring it. The difficulties encountered by Mrs. Thatcher's government in trying to reduce the size of the public sector tell a very illuminating story in this respect.

Furthermore, the benefits of a reduction in the size of government are not visible, in the sense that they are not directly and immediately experienced, but must be imagined.[20] The costs of a given reduction in government spending, on the other hand, are quite visible: they usually take the form of a reduction in currently enjoyed consumption. It is, therefore, easier for people to understand the case for government spending than it is to understand the case for its reduction. Even though, as we have just mentioned, a number of recent electoral outcomes seem to indicate a general preference for a reduction in the size of government, it is uncertain whether it will be possible to implement policies aimed at achieving that result. When the problem will move from the general case for less government to reducing particular categories of public spending, resistance to such a move might prove to be impossible to overcome.[21]

In light of the above argument, therefore, it is not entirely unreasonable to argue that pressures favoring the growth of government have often their origin in the voters' behavior, and that, even though a substantial democratic majority might come to favor a reduction in the size of government, it is far from clear that such a reduction will prove to be feasible.

The Politician

From what we have said about the voters it is very easy to see how this in turn affects the structure of incentives for the politicians. One need not have "an irrational passion for dispassionate rationality" in order to argue that politicians in a democracy aim at maximizing their chances of reelection. After all, it is a fact of common observation that most politicians behave in such a way as to please their constituents, on whose votes their political future crucially depends. Nor is it all bad that things should be so. After all, democracy is based on the principle that politicians are servants of the people, that they should do what their electors ask them to do. As a result, even though a politician might be convinced that a further expansion of the size of government is detrimental to society as whole, he is unlikely to resist a specific spending project that benefits his constituents while damaging the whole of society. Indeed, chances are that he is going to be a strong supporter of such a spending project, while possibly at the same time advocating a *general* reduction in government spending (a reduction, that is, that falls not on his electors but on others). It is for this reason that Parliaments, whose historical *raison d'être* was the need to resist the spending and taxing proposals of the sovereign, have now become big spenders of the people's money. Indeed, in some cases, it is not uncommon for politicians to boast of their success in introducing legislation that favors their constituency at the expense of general revenue, and to point to this fact as a valid reason for people to vote for them. The traditional role of Parliament is, in such a way, turned upside down: instead of providing a check on public spending, it promotes the growth of government expenditure.

Furthermore, quite often projects that do not have majority support in Parliament end up being approved thanks to the practice of logrolling, which allows a majority to be formed by assembling several minorities favoring different spending proposals. Thus, mass democracy quite often means that spending proposals that are opposed by a majority of the people end up being implemented thanks to a majority of votes in Parliament made up of the coalition of several minority pressure groups.

The above consideration should dispose of the common fallacy that in a democracy the size of government is determined by the people's preferences. According to this notion there could be no such thing as excessive government. From what we have said, however, it should be clear that the fact that politicians ask for increases in spending in response to the request of their voters does not mean that for every spending proposal there is a majority favoring it, nor that the existing ratio of public sector spending to national income is that which would be chosen by a majority of the voters in a popular referendum. The possibility of forming majorities by adding several minorities, in fact, means that it is possible to implement projects that a majority of the voters would oppose. Rather than being based on a majority rule, unlimited democracy seems to be based on a system of compromises that allows Parliament to systematically introduce legislation that the majority would oppose.

The Taxpayer

The taxpayer bears the cost of government growth. As we have seen, as people become aware of the increased cost of government, they try to resist it in various ways, either by supporting parties and politicians who promise to limit the scope of government and to cut taxes, or by way of popular referenda like Proposition 13 in California.

Taxpayers' resistance, however, is not always successful. For the reasons stated above, electing politicians who promise to cut taxes and reducing government spending is often an insufficient condition for achieving the desired result. The structure of incentives, as we have seen, is such that it discourages the actual implementation of policies aimed at taming government. Furthermore, in many countries the option of a popular referendum is not available, so that taxpayers' resistance lacks the means to translate itself into effective political pressure.[22] It is not unlikely that such an impotence of taxpayers to resist the confiscatory policies made inevitable by the growth of government is one of the major forces behind the growth of tax avoidance and evasion in many countries.

In the case of Italy, as in that of other countries, moreover, taxpayers' resistance is prevented by another, more fundamental, consideration. In order for taxpayers to oppose government growth, they must be aware of the share of the cost of government that falls on them. People, that is, must realize that *they* are paying for government spending; they must be aware of how much they are paying in taxes. In order for that to happen, taxes must be *visible*, so that people know how much they are paying. While this is true of some kinds of taxes, it is not true for all. Obviously, from the point of view of the government and of the politicians the preferred type of tax is that which people pay without realizing, for that avoids the possibility of tax resistance and leaves people unaware of the cost of government. In Italy, most taxes are of this kind.

That the distinguishing feature of the Italian tax system is its lack of transparency can be easily understood by looking at the tax structure. In 1978 income tax revenue amounted to 11.4 percent of national income—a rather "low" figure, possibly reflecting substantial tax evasion. However, the important point is that most of the revenue from the income tax is paid in the form of withholding, and people are used to thinking of their income in terms of the net figure, without considering the amount their employer has had to turn over to the taxman. Indirect taxes amounted to 11.3 percent of national income and, again, people pay these taxes without realizing it. For instance, the price of gasoline was 750 lire a liter (roughly $3.20 per gallon at the 1980 exchange rate), of which some 500 lire was sales tax: two thirds! Most people are not aware of this, and they tend to attribute the exorbitant price of gas entirely to the greed of Arab sheiks and multinational oil companies.

To income taxes and indirect taxes one must add social security taxes, which in 1978 amounted to 15.7 percent of national income. Again, people are seldom aware of paying these taxes as they are generally withheld by their employer. To the 38.4 percent of "explicit"

49

taxes one must add the 15.3 percent of the hidden tax of government deficit, which very few people indeed perceive as a tax, tending rather to put the blame for inflation and unemployment on a variety of scapegoats ranging from labor unions to "capitalism." This general lack of transparency of the Italian tax system explains how a country of ingenious tax evaders can end up sacrificing 53.7 percent of its income (in 1978) to the greed of bureaucrats and politicians.[23]

What interests us here is that the lack of transparency prevents active taxpayers' resistance in the traditional form, for people are not aware of how much of their income is being taken from them by the government. It is a safe bet that, if Italians were aware of the exact amount of taxes they are paying, they would put up widespread resistance to the size of government and promote the kind of political change that might promise to curb government growth. Finally, the fact that "Italy has been the leader in non-payment of taxes" and that the Italian underground economy seems to be flourishing can be interpreted as an effective, albeit illegal, form of taxpayers' resistance.[24]

In the light of the preceding considerations, it should be evident that the system of political incentives is unbalanced: it is biased in favor of government growth. While voters and politicians are motivated by the incentives structure to press for increased public spending, taxpayers are often unaware of what they are paying and/or unable to exert the kind of political pressure that might succeed in preventing further government growth.[25]

The situation had been clearly understood by the great Italian economist Vilfredo Pareto, who, almost a century ago, wrote:

> Let us suppose that in a country of thirty million inhabitants it is proposed, under some pretext or other, to get each citizen to pay out one franc a year, and to distribute the total amount amongst thirty persons. Every one of the donors will give up one franc a year; every one of the beneficiaries will receive one million francs a year. The two groups will differ very greatly in their response to this situation. Those who hope to gain a million a year will know no rest by day or night. They will win newspapers over to their interest by financial inducements and drum up support from all quarters. A discreet hand will warm the palms of needy legislators, even of ministers. . . . On the other hand, the despoiled are much less active. A great deal of money is needed to launch an electoral campaign. Now there are insuperable material difficulties militating against asking each citizen to contribute a few centimes. One has to ask a few people to make substantial contributions. But then, for such people, there is the likelihood that their individual contribution to the campaign against the spoliation will exceed the total amount they stand to lose by the measure in question. . . . When election day comes, similar difficulties are encountered. Those who hope to gain a million apiece have agents everywhere, who descend in swarms on the electorate, urg-

ing the voters that sound and enlightened patriotism calls for the success of their modest proposal. They will go further if need be, and are quite prepared to lay out cash to get the necessary votes for returning candidates in their interest. In contrast, the individual who is threatened with losing one franc a year — even if he is fully aware of what is afoot — will not for so small a thing forego a picnic in the country, or fall out with useful or congenial friends, or get on the wrong side of the mayor or the *préfet*! In these circumstances the outcome is not in doubt: the spoliators will win hands down.[26]

Pareto's "structuralist" explanation of government growth has thus been summarized by Professor James M. Buchanan:

> Beneficiary groups, recipients of direct transfers or of governmentally-financed programs, tend to be concentrated, organized, and capable of exerting influence over elected politicians. By contrast, taxpayer groups, those who pay taxes, tend to be widely dispersed and, indeed, tend to include almost everyone due to the fact that taxes are general rather than specific. As a result of the asymmetry, it becomes easier to get political decision-makers to expand budgets than to contract them. There is a structural bias toward expanded levels of taxation and spending, and this bias has become increasingly pronounced as governments have invented and discovered new ways of spending.

> Within the budget itself, there is a comparable bias toward outlays that provide direct benefits to concentrated groups as opposed to outlays (e.g., national defense) that provide benefits over the whole citizenry.[27]

Business and Labor

The preceding analysis of the political process under conditions of unlimited democracy goes a long way in explaining the bias in favor of government growth that afflicts most Western democracies. Government intervention, on the other hand, reinforces the tendency toward bigger government in an indirect way, by distorting the working of the system of industrial relations. This is true of both businessmen and labor leaders.

It is generally believed that businessmen tend to be "conservative", that they support, that is, a free-enterprise system based on limited government. As is often the case with generally held beliefs, the statement is wrong to a very large extent. Businessmen often do pay lip service to the virtues of competition and free enterprise. However, this is true mostly of successful businessmen. As soon as they begin to experience difficulties with the conduct of their business, entrepreneurs are strongly tempted to ask for government help, either in the form of subsidies, or import controls, or in a variety of other ways. In a free market economy, based on the principle of personal responsibility,

51

such a temptation is usually constrained by the capitalistic ethic according to which people bear the consequences of their decisions. If a businessman succeeds, that is, he is entitled to the profit he makes, and by the same token, if he fails, he must bear the consequences of his failure.

In Italy, the ethic of capitalism was first undermined by Mussolini's economic policy, which was often based on the idea that government should support industry. The effects of this fascist idea—so dear to some contemporary businessmen and leftist intellectuals—were well summarized by Gaetano Salvemini, when he wrote: "In actual fact, it is the State, i.e., the taxpayer, who has become responsible to private enterprise. In Fascist Italy the State pays for the blunders of private enterprise....Profit is private and individual. Loss is public and social."[28]

The results of such a policy in terms of economic efficiency are devastating. What happens is that the government subsidizes failures (successful businesses don't need any subsidies), thereby preventing the needed transformations in the industrial structure, delaying growth, and producing misallocation of resources on a large scale. A good illustration is provided by the performance of IRI (Istituto per la Ricostruzione Industriale), which is Italy's giant state holding. IRI has at times been quoted as a successful mixture of socialism and capitalism. While few people seem to remember that such a mixture is a fascist invention—for IRI was born then—it is very hard to see where IRI's success is. From June 1977 to June 1978 IRI has lost 722 billion lire, approximately 1.5 million lire ($1,830 at the then prevailing exchange rate) for every worker employed. It is worth stressing that IRI is Europe's largest industrial employer, with over 500,000 employees, so that its failure is not a minor accident. So far, it has accumulated debts for 30,000 billion lire, or $34 billion, i.e., over $65,000 for every worker employed.

What concerns us here is that the economic policy of "bailing out" businesses that are experiencing economic difficulties is a contagious disease. Not only does it tend to spread inefficiency throughout the economic system, distorting the allocation of resources and delaying growth, but it also provides businessmen with an incentive to advocate government intervention when it suits their interest. As a result, businessmen have become vociferous supporters of government growth in countries, such as Italy and Great Britain, that have adopted such a policy.

The point of view of the businessman is not difficult to understand: he is obviously delighted at the prospect of an economic system that allows him to retain his profits when things go well, and pays for his losses when things go wrong. It is also easy to understand how businessmen can succeed in selling such a policy to politicians. All they need to do is to hint that failure to bail that particular business out would result in the unemployment of the workers engaged in it. Such a strategy seldom fails to impress politicians, as they are understandably quite sensitive to the political costs of publicly refusing to prevent the unemployment that would result from that business' failure.

It might be worth adding that such a policy violates the basic principle of personal responsibility, which is the very essence of a free market economy, and it inevitably results in economic inefficiency and the sclerosis of the productive system. More important from our point of view, such a policy has transformed businessmen as a group into ardent advocates of increased government spending "in support" of industry. The interesting aspect of it is that the two traditional adversaries of the system of industrial relations — business and labor — have become accomplices in asking the government to subsidize their joint inefficiency.

Direct government intervention in the economy has also had devastating effects on the behavior of labor unions, for it has encouraged — indeed rewarded — union aggressiveness and irresponsibility. From this point of view, the "wage push" in Italy must be seen as an indirect effect of the more general government push.

In a free market economy, the natural instinct of labor unions to push for higher and higher wages is offset by a variety of constraints. First of all, the unions' demand for higher wages is met by the natural reluctance of businessmen to grant excessive wage increases that would endanger the survival of their enterprise. Furthermore, union leaders are constrained by the fear that their action will result in very high rates of unemployment. They are well aware of the fact that whereas inflation tends to strengthen their hold on their members and their bargaining power, unemployment tends to weaken this hold. It is hard to tell on *a priori* grounds whether the system of collective bargaining is symmetrically balanced, but there is no doubt that in the context of a free market economy there are potentially effective constraints on the labor unions' bargaining power. Collective bargaining takes place between two *responsible* parties, who must bear the consequences of their action: a businessman who grants an excessive wage increase will end up experiencing financial difficulties and ultimately bankruptcy; unions who push for excessive wage increases will have to put up with the resulting unemployment of many of their members.

This system of constraints has been destroyed by government growth with the result that collective bargaining takes place in a framework of general irresponsibility, so that it is now referred to as "free collective chaos."[29]

The destruction of the discipline of the market has been accomplished in two ways. On the one hand, the policies of subsidizing "problem firms" and of the government replacing unsuccessful businessmen have weakened the management's resistance to excessive wage claims. As we have mentioned before, this has resulted in wage negotiations which take place between trade unions asking for excessive wage increases and managers of public firms willingly surrendering "public"—i.e., taxpayer's—money to the unions in order to buy "social peace". On the other hand, the government's commitment to a mistaken interpretation of "full employment" has meant that businesses are prevented from closing down by the policy of government bail out. As a result, trade unions no longer have to deal with the possibility that their exhorbitant wage claims might result in unemployment. Since the government has assumed responsibility for full employment, labor leaders know that they can successfully blame any unemployment that might result from their action on the government's inability to achieve its goal. In Italy, political factors add to the aggressiveness of trade unions, which has resulted from such a distortion in the system of industrial relations, because trade unions leaders are often commited to marxist ideology and do not hide the fact that their ultimate goal is the "destruction of the system" and its replacement with a socialist society.

The effects of such a policy on the unions' aggressiveness are vividly illustrated by the figures on strikes. These have become such a common feature that Italy has earned the nickname of "strikeland". The label is entirely appropriate: the average number of days of strike per 1,000 workers per year from 1963 to 1978 has been five times higher in Italy than in the other EEC countries. (See Table 6)

Although there obviously are other factors accounting for the sharp difference in unions' aggressiveness between Italy and the other European countries, the figures in Table 6 are all the more remarkable because they do not refer to a short period of time, when contingent, exceptional factors might be prevalent, but account for a 15-year period, so that the influence of exceptional factors should play an insignificant role.

Another indicator of the trade unions' aggressiveness is the rate of growth of nominal wages, which has been higher in Italy than in any other EEC country.[30]

The unconstrained power of the labor unions runs counter to the logic of the Italian Constitution, which devotes two articles to the problem of the discipline of strikes and labor unions organization. However, the two articles have never been enforced.[31]

The aggressiveness of the Italian trade unions is the expected, inevitable consequence of an economic policy that has disposed of the discipline of the market and condemned collective bargaining to be governed

Table 6
Number of working days lost through industrial stoppages,
per 1,000 employees, per year. 1963–1978 average.

Luxembourg	0.0
Holland	36.2
W. Germany	47.3
Denmark	206.3
Belgium	274.8
France	284.0
United Kingdom	499.8
Ireland	924.7
Italy	1,412.9

Source: Eurostat, *Occupazione e Disoccupazione,* July 1979.

by the interplay of symmetrical irresponsibilities. It is highly doubtful, therefore, that the problem could simply be solved by legislative action, as long as the interventionist policy continues.

Such a policy has transformed businessmen and labor union leaders into powerful pressure groups favoring increased government spending. It is not that wage increases indirectly persuade the Central Bank to pursue an expansionary monetary policy in order to prevent widespread unemployment. What happens is that the system of collective irresponsibility results in excessive wage increases; these, in turn, create financial difficulties for some firms, who turn to the government for help. The joint pressures exercised by both management and labor in favor of a bail out proves politically irresistible. The business losses find their way into the government budget and, together with the losses of the already *public* sector, result in increases in the government deficit. When the size of the deficit exceeds some critical percentage of national income, it becomes literally impossible to finance it by genuine borrowing from the market. Debt monetization, i.e., money creation, becomes the inevitable alternative. Thus, monetary folly and inflation are nothing but the expected outcome of the government push, which entails collective irresponsibility in wage bargaining, and which, together with the working of the system of political incentives in favor of government growth, produces huge government deficits that cannot be financed in a non-inflationary way.

The government push, in other words, makes it difficult to distinguish and separate the various components of the mechanism of inflationary finance, because it tends to influence wages, government deficits, and money creation simultaneously.

The Keynesian Revolution

At this point, a problem arises. The incentives structure affecting the behavior of voters, politicians, and taxpayers in such a way as to promote government growth can be assumed to have been in existence ever since mass democracy was born. Why is it, then, that the most visible sign of the government push—government deficits—did not start to increase in the Italian economy until the early 1960s? In other words, even if we limit our analysis to the post-World War II period, when mass democracy was introduced in Italy, it is evident from the figures on the government deficit previously given that the period preceding the 1960s was immune from the growth in the deficit that took place after that. And yet, nothing in our analysis of the structure of incentives says why this should be so: if it is valid, it should apply equally to the 1950s and to the following two decades. What prevented it from working in the 1950s?

The first possible answer is that mentioned above: in the early 1960s a change in the government coalition took place, with the birth of the "center-left" government. The inclusion of the Italian Socialist Party (PSI) meant a move toward a policy of increased government intervention in the economy and rapidly growing public spending. But the political change was only the visible symptom of a drastic change in the philosophy of government that followed the "Keynesian revolution" in economic thought. This meant a completely different approach to the fiscal responsibility of government from the one that had prevailed in the 1950s. As a consequence of the influence of Keynesian orthodoxy, there was an "inflation of government" and a resulting inflationary bias in the financial structure.

The fact that Keynesian theory tends to attach little importance to the role of money in the determination of economic activity has already been mentioned.

An indirect effect of the Keynesian approach to the role of money is that Keynesian economists tend to pay little attention to monetary policy in general, concentrating rather on fiscal—i.e., budget—policy, and "real", as opposed to monetary, factors. They probably do not go as far as to say that "money does not matter," but they have consistently adhered to the notion that it matters very little. The neglect of the importance of money in the determination of aggregate spending is in itself an element of the inflationary bias of Keynesian economic policies, because it prevents them from understanding the origin and nature of the inflationary process. Other factors, however, contribute to the inflationary bias of Keynesian policies.

The first such factor is the belief in the exogenous nature of the price level and of the inflation rate. The idea is that prices are what they are, determined by institutional or historical factors, and that demand management should accordingly aim at making full employment real income possible at that—exogenously determined—price level. A variation of this approach is given by the extraordinary importance attached to the goal of "full employment" and the relatively minor attention devoted to that of price stability. No less an authority than Sir John Hicks has summed up this perspective by saying that "the view which emerges from *The General Theory* is more radical than 'full employment without inflation'; it is nothing less than the view that inflation does not matter..."[32]

The relative neglect of the danger of inflation was probably due to the circumstances of the time *The General Theory* was written. The situation Keynes had in mind was one of insufficient aggregate demand, widespread unemployment, and idle productive capacity. Under those circumstances, the danger was that of deflation, generally falling prices and rising inventories of unsold products, rather than inflation. Therefore, it was easy to come to the conclusion that inflation was unlikely to occur and to concentrate rather on the need to stimulate aggregate spending.

The second factor which accounts for the inflationary bias in Keynesian policies is the idea that nominal wage rates were rigid downward. This leads to the belief that excessively high nominal wages leading to unemployment could be corrected by price rises. In other words, if the nominal wage rises to a level that is incompatible with full employment, the solution must be found not in a reduction of the nominal wage, for that is impossible, but in an increase in prices that reduces the real value of the wage rate and brings it back to its equilibrium level. As Keynes himself stated:

> It is fortunate that the workers, though unconsciously, are instinctively more reasonable economists than the classical school, inasmuch as they resist reductions of money-wages, which are seldom or never of an all-round character,...whereas they do not resist reductions of real wages, which are associated with increases in aggregate employment and leave relative money-wages unchanged....[33]

Inflation, therefore, is seen by Keynesian economists not only as unlikely, but even as beneficial in that it is an instrument of a full-employment policy, a way to reconcile conflicting wage claims, of restoring real wages to their equilibrium levels. Little attention is paid to the fact that workers are interested in the *real* value of their wages and are unlikely to be fooled by an economic policy that takes away from them through inflation what they have succeeded in getting through collective bargaining. Of course, as long as inflation is unexpected, it catches workers by surprise and succeeds in reducing the real value of excessive wage increases. But, sooner or later, workers catch up with the reality of the inflationary process and it becomes increasingly difficult to fool them. In Italy, this is how escalator clauses have become widespread, linking the wage rate to the price index and thereby protecting its real value against the inflationary erosion. At that point, inflation loses its stimulating power and it has little, if any, positive effect on employment levels. Keynesian economists, however, have been singularly impervious to this kind of problem until the second half of the 1970s, and have, therefore, preferred to stick to the notion that inflation was not only unlikely and unrelated to demand policies, but beneficial in terms of employment levels.

A third factor accounting for the inflationary bias in Keynesian policies is the idea that, as long as there is unused productive capacity, one cannot talk of inflation. This view suggests that the increase in prices and wages that is associated with an expansion of economic activity does not amount to inflation, and that one can talk of inflation only after full employment has been attained. Given the fact that we do not have a satisfactory definition of full employment, and that some degree of unemployment will always be present, such a notion amounts to saying that inflation proper does not exist.

Paradoxically, such a notion was stressed by Keynes in an article devoted to warning English public opinion of the danger of inflation:

> ...what do we mean by 'inflation'? If we mean by the term a state of affairs which is dangerous and ought to be avoided...then we must not mean by it merely that prices and wages are rising. For a rising tendency of prices and wages inevitably...accompanies any revival of activity.
> ...It is when increased demand is no longer capable of materially raising output and employment and mainly spends itself in raising prices that it is properly called inflation.[34]

As we have seen, Keynes' obsession with the short run was also doomed to result in both de-stabilizing macroeconomic policies and in an inflationary bias.

Another factor that might have played a role in the inflationary bias of Keynesianism is that Keynes' view of the economy in simple macroeconomic terms tended to ignore the distortion of relative prices that inevitably accompanies a change in the price level. The disruptive effect of inflation on the working of the price system and on the allocation of resources was accordingly given little attention by Keynesian economists, who could not, therefore, understand the negative consequences of inflation.

But the most important factor accounting for the inflationary bias of Keynesianism, and the one that explains the explosion of the budget deficit after the advent of the "Keynesian revolution" in Italy, is the fact that Keynesianism has destroyed the most effective constraint on government growth. In the period preceding the Keynesian revolution, all the incentives toward government growth were present in the working of the Italian mass democracy, but they were kept in check by the "orthodox" belief that government deficits were a symptom of financial irresponsibility in the conduct of public affairs. Just as a private individual or a family was to try to limit expenses so as not to exceed income, governments were supposed to try to balance their budget. Their failure to do so was considered an inexcusable manifestation of financial irresponsibility; governments were proud of any reduction in the deficit and apologetic about any increase. As we have seen, such a constraint worked very well in the 1950s in Italy: from 1951 to 1962 (the "liberal" era), the government deficit declined from 388 to 357 billion lire in nominal terms, from almost 4 percent of GNP to 1.5 percent! It was then that the political change took place and the new orthodoxy of Keynesianism replaced the old wisdom. The effect on the deficit, as we have seen, was explosive: from 1962 to 1980, the deficit has gone from 1.5 to 11.6 percent of GNP.

Keynesianism has provided governments with a theoretical justification for their irresponsibility: a balanced budget was no longer a goal of economic policy, a good thing, but a symptom of old fashioned myths in economic thinking.

It must be stressed, however, that Keynes did not advocate a government deficit under all circumstances. His view was rather that a private enterprise, free market economy was inherently unstable and that it was possible to remedy the instability by compensatory variations in the government budget. It was the responsibility of the government to manipulate the budget so as to produce a deficit when aggregate spending fell short of full employment real income, and produce a surplus when there was an excess of aggregate spending.

> The policy precepts of Keynesian economics were alleged to be wholly symmetrical. In depressed economic conditions, budget deficits would be required to restore full employment and prosperity. When inflation threatened, budget surpluses would be appropriate. The time-honoured norm of budget balance was thus jettisoned, but, in the pure logic Keynesian policy, there was no one-way departure. It might even be said that Keynesian economics did not destroy the principle of a balanced budget, but only lengthened the time-period over which it applied, from a calendar year to the period of a business cycle.[35]

From what we have said, however, it is easy to see why Keynes' anti-cyclical prescriptions were doomed to be applied only in one direction. First of all, there always is some degree of unemployment for a variety of reasons. Keynesian economists can then use existing unemployment figures as evidence of insufficient aggregate spending and in support of the need for deficit spending. Second, as we have stressed, Keynesianism also amounted to insensitivity to the problem of inflation. This meant that a policy aimed at budget surpluses was never advocated, because inflation was not perceived to be a problem. The only desirable policy was that of a budget deficit, which was supposed to be expansionary.

But the main reason why Keynesian economic policy was doomed to be interpreted as recommending the desirability of increasing government deficits has to do with what we have said about the incentives structure in the political process of an unlimited democracy. As we have seen, the situation is such that it makes the interest of elected politicians directly connected to government growth. Whereas before Keynes such a powerful incentive to the government push was offset by the balanced-budget philosophy, after the acceptance of Keynesian policy prescriptions the constraint was removed. In the old order, any increase in spending had to be accompanied by an increase in taxes, in order for the budget to be balanced. As we have seen, just as spending is politically profitable, taxing is politically unpopular. The incentive to spend more in order to increase one's popularity was therefore offset by the need to increase taxes in order to finance the new project. Once the need to balance the budget was removed, no check on the incentives structure was left. There was no reason why government spending should not keep on growing, without even increasing explicit taxes in order to finance it. As we shall see in the next chapter, a by-product of the new philosophy is that it has separated spending decisions from taxing decisions. This is true in the United Kingdom:

> As Sir Alec Cairncross has said, we are the only country in the world where decisions about expenditure are taken before decisions about taxation. The two should obviously be taken together....[36]

This is unfortunately even more so in Italy, as evidenced by the size of the deficit, and this is, as we shall see in the next chapter, somewhat paradoxical because it openly violates the Italian Constitution.

The further, unintended consequence of separating taxing and spending decisions is that it is impossible for politicians to be aware of the true cost of their spending decisions. Since the two are taken in isolation, Parliament operates under the delusion that government spending is costless, for the social desirability of a given project is never compared to the other desirable alternatives that have to be foregone in order to implement it.

As a result, the Italian case provides strong evidence in support of J. M. Buchanan and R. E. Wagner's view:

> The grafting of Keynesian economics onto the fabric of a political democracy has wrought a significant revision in the underlying fiscal constitution. The result has been a tendency toward budget deficits and, consequently, once the workings of democratic political institutions are taken into account, inflation. Democratic governments will generally respond more vigorously in correcting for unemployment than in correcting for inflation....Budget deficits will come to be the general rule, even when inflation is severe....Moreover, the perceived cost of gov-

ernment will generally be lower than the real cost because of the deficit financing. As a consequence, there will also be a relative increase in the size of the government sector in the economy. Budget deficits, inflation, and the growth of government—all are intensified by the Keynesian destruction of former constitutional principles of sound finance. (p. 23)

The mounting historical evidence of the ill-effects of Keynes's ideas cannot continue to be ignored. Keynesian economics has turned the politicians loose; it has destroyed the effective constraint on politicians' ordinary appetites to spend and spend without the apparent necessity to tax.

Sober assessment suggests that, politically, Keynesianism represents a substantial disease that over the long run can prove fatal for the survival of democracy. (p. 27)[37]

Before we leave the impact of the Keynesian revolution on the economic policies in Italy, mention must be made of a somewhat related negative consequence of government growth and inflation. We have seen that inflation was perceived by Keynes as a way to reconcile conflicting wage claims, of restoring real wage rates to their equilibrium level, and of protecting full employment. In this perspective, inflation is seen as a factor of social peace; a peaceful way to remedy the consequences of excessive wage increases without having to risk a confrontation with the labor unions. We have also said that it is impossible to "fool all of the people all of the time" in the sense that, as soon as labor unions become aware of the reality of the inflationary process, they will protect themselves against the erosion of the real value of their wages brought about by inflation. Escalator clauses, linking wages to the cost of living index, are the device used to a large extent in Italy to achieve that result. The introduction of escalator clauses on a large scale has meant that inflation has no stimulating power in terms of employment. There is no trade-off between inflation and unemployment, at least not in the positive sense Keynesian economists have been maintaining for the past two decades.

Unfortunately, this is not the end of the story. The high inflation rates produced by the government push have also created the conditions for the disruption of the social fabric, despite extensive indexation (or perhaps because of the way it has been introduced). What I am referring to is the dramatic distortion in the relative income structure within the public sector that has been produced by the combined effect of inflation and biased indexation. The type of indexation in Italy is biased in favor of manual workers and against clerical employees. The first group's income is more than compensated for inflation, whereas that of the second group is less than protected. As a result, inflation has resulted in the relative impoverishment of university-educated, middle class government employees, who understandably re-

61

sent the deterioration of their position in the distributive scale. Despite (or because of) extensive indexation, inflation has produced the familiar result of undesirable redistribution with its accompanying by-products of envy, resentment, and social tensions.

For example, the monthly salary of an average blue-collar worker in the public sector equalled 187,674 lire in January 1975; five years later, in December 1979, it was 476,388 lire. In five years, it has increased from 100 to 253.8, whereas the cost-of-living index has increased only from 100 to 199.4. On the other hand, the salary of a highly qualified white collar executive in the government bureaucracy has gone from 345,478 lire to 540,818 lire: from 200 to 156.5. In other words, whereas the blue collar worker's salary has increased 27.3 percent *in real terms* from 1975 to 1979, the real salary of the government executive has *declined* by 21.5 percent during the same period.[38] Inflation, far from bringing about social peace, is creating the conditions for an explosive confrontation and the ultimate destruction of the social fabric. Such a consideration obviously reinforces Buchanan and Wagner's gloomy prediction about the incompatibility of inflationary government with the survival of a free democracy.

The Time Horizon

The powerful mechanism of incentives favoring the growth of government is further strengthened, in the case of Italy, by the high instability of the executive. From 1946 to 1980, Italy has had thirty-nine different governments. This means that the average life expectancy of a government in Italy is less than one year. Understandably, this leads to a myopic approach on the part of government to economic policies. It is a known fact that the immediate, short run effects of a decrease in public spending are likely to be painful. Some government employees lose their jobs, firms that were working for the public sector lose their contracts and beneficiaries of transfer payments see their benefits reduced or nullified, and so on. On the other hand, the beneficial effects of a reduction in government spending come later: it takes time for new productive activities to replace the government project, and still more time for the new investments to increase the overall rate of economic growth. A government that would engage in a reduction in spending would be likely to be blamed for the immediate, painful side effects of the decision and, given the short life expectancy of government in Italy, would not be credited with the long run beneficial effects of the reduction.

In other words, the time horizon in the government's decision-making process is of necessity conditioned by its expected duration in power. A government that expects to stay in power for less than one year is unlikely to pay attention to the consequences of its decisions that will materialize beyond its existence. It will then, naturally, favor decisions that produce their beneficial effects soon, even though they might have detrimental consequences in the distant future. This is true of increases in government spending: their immediate effect is that of creating the impression that the government is "doing something" to promote desirable economic goals. Jobs are "created", benefits are handed out, and profits are distributed. The popularity of the existing government is enhanced. Furthermore, in choosing among competing spending projects, governments will tend to favor those that have an immediate, even if short-lived, impact, and neglect those that permanently increase the productive capacity of the country. The world of government economic decision-making becomes a world of crickets, centered on trying to get the most out of the present and entirely oblivious to the future.

The same asymmetry in the time perspective operates in the field of monetary policy, because inflation produces its "beneficial" effects immediately, whereas its painful consequences show up later. On the other hand, an anti-inflationary monetary policy has painful side effects in the near future, whereas the long-lasting gains come at a later stage. As a result, a government that has a short life expectancy will naturally favor inflationary decisions and oppose any anti-inflationary action. This leads Willett and Laney to say:

> Despite the readily apparent costs of short time horizon in macroeconomic decision making it is an open question whether the adoption of longer time horizons will prove politically feasible.[39]

For our present purposes the important point is that the contrast between short run political gains and long run economic damages of policy decisions translates itself into an additional factor of government growth. In addition, the short time horizon makes inflation a politically palatable and attractive way to finance such a growth, which further diminishes the prospects for the adoption of an effective anti-inflationary policy.

It is hard to tell on *a priori* grounds if the problem of the time horizon can be solved by the choice of a constitutional device designed to guarantee that governments last for an appropriate length of time. Even countries that have less unstable political systems than Italy face similar problems. Some economies are allegedly behaving according to a "political cycle", determined by the interplay of electoral deadlines and economic policy decisions based on electoral considerations.[40] In other words, even though the myopic approach to economic policy is strengthened by political instability, as in Italy, the existence of a "political business cycle" suggests that increasing the life expectancy of

63

the government does not make economic policy decisions immune from electoral considerations. The solution must be found elsewhere, and it must aim at eliminating short-run influences from the economic policy decision-making process.

The Vicious Circle of Irresponsibility

What we have said about the Italian system of political incentives to government growth should explain what was meant when excessive increases in the quantity of money were singled out as a *proximate* cause of inflation. The fact is that monetary growth is itself a symptom of deeper factors. These are typical of all "mixed" economies in political democracies, although to a different extent. If the Italian situation presents symptoms of economic decay that are unequalled in some other Western democracies, this only means that the Italian disease is more extreme, but it does not mean that other countries are immune from it. Inflation, too rapid growth of the quantity of money, rising budget deficits, and accelerating government growth, are all typical of almost all Western democracies. If this is the case, then much can be learned from observing a more advanced case of the same disease.

The factors behind excessively rapid monetary growth are, as we have seen, related to the structure of incentives favoring government growth in political democracies. I have elsewhere referred to such a situation as the vicious circle of irresponsibility.[41] We have seen how the distorted perception of costs and benefits of government spending accounts for the fact that voters' resistance to government growth is much less strong than their pressures in favor of the enactment of new spending projects. The reason is simply that they are not aware that the costs of government growth fall on them. They behave, therefore, as if they were irresponsible, as if someone else would bear the consequences of their actions in favor of government growth. We have also seen that for the individual voter (or group of voters) this lack of perception is not due to irrationality. On the contrary, the behavior of individual pressure groups is dictated by a correct interpretation of their own private self interest, and it is perfectly rational. The fact is that what is true for the individual voter (or group of voters) is not true for society as a whole. The combined effect of the pressures coming from pressure groups correctly pursuing their self interest eventually results in a situation in which everybody loses.

In a democracy, elected politicians are (should be) sensitive to their electors' wishes and desires. The fact that politicians respond to pressures favoring government growth that come from their constituents is what one would normally expect from democratic representatives of the people. If they do not resist government growth, therefore, this

64

cannot be blamed on them. Even if they are convinced that government growth is detrimental to society as a whole, why should they be held responsible for voicing support for particular government projects that benefit their own constituents? Should we expect them to behave in such a way as to destroy their chances for reelection? What is democratic about a politician who deliberately ignores his constituents' wishes? Politicians, like voters, cannot be held responsible for the growth of government.

Similarly, labor unions pushing for excessive wage increases cannot be held responsible for the economic consequences of their actions. Their duty is that of pursuing the interest of their members as they perceive it. No one has entrusted them with the responsibility to protect economic stability. If they behave in a way that is incompatible with price stability and full employment, the blame must be given not to them but to statism. Government intervention has meant, as we have seen, the end of responsible collective bargaining. When the government assumes responsibility for full employment, this relieves the unions from the need of considering the unemployment of their members that might result from excessive wage increases. The natural constraint on unions' behavior is thus removed. No wonder they try to get as much as possible in terms of wage increases and fringe benefits. On the other hand, direct government intervention in the economy removes another constraint on unions' behavior, by making management less reluctant to grant excessive wage increases: managerial irresponsibility in the public sector enhances trade unions' irresponsibility. Finally, the policy of "bailing out" problem firms makes even private businessmen less responsive to market signals and removes the most effective constraint on their behavior: bankruptcy. Business and labor irresponsibility combine in asking for greater government spending in the form of higher wages and subsidies to ailing firms. However, both businessmen and labor union leaders behave according to their own self interest as they perceive it. Why blame *them*? The culprit is, obviously, an economic policy that has destroyed the discipline of the market and spread irresponsibility throughout the economy.

Parliament is not responsible for what is happening. There is no law prohibiting the formation of a majority in Parliament based on the addition of several minorities. Furthermore, in the Italian case, an electoral system based on proportional representation has resulted in a large number of political parties in Parliament. No single party, therefore, has ever had a majority of votes in Parliament since 1948. The only way to form a majority is that of a coalition of several (minority) parties. This is how legislation favoring special groups is approved even if opposed by the majority of the people, but, in Italy at least, such an outcome is naturally tied to proportional representation.

Once again, however, such an outcome is not peculiar to Italy. Even in countries that do not have a multi-party system and that are governed by a party possessing a clear majority of votes, legislation favored by small but active minorities is enacted thanks to the practice of logrolling. Several minorities, each interested in a special project, combine together to form the kind of majority that is needed to pass the legislation they favor. Each single project is strictly a minority one — one, that is, that would not receive a majority of votes in a popular referendum — but, taken together, the various minorities add up and succeed in getting their favored legislation enacted.

As a result, government spending grows beyond the level that would be favored by the majority of voters in a public referendum. The question then becomes: who is responsible for such an undemocratic outcome? The answer is that, in Italy at least, no one is responsible. Labor unions and Parliament are not responsible for pushing for higher wages and more government spending, for they do so in response to pressures coming from the people they represent (union members and groups of voters). The government is not responsible for not resisting the pressures coming from Parliament; after all, Italy is a parliamentary democracy and the government derives its power from a parliamentary majority. The Minister of the Budget is not responsible, for the size of the deficit does not depend on his autonomous decisions, but is largely determined by commitments made by Parliament. The monetary authorities are not responsible, because, given the size of the public deficit, they must pay for it and this severely limits their control over the money supply. As a result of this vicious circle of irresponsibility, money creation is neither trusted to some set rule, as would be advisable, nor controlled by the monetary authorities.

The resulting sustained inflation is what had to be expected. When the quantity of money grows at the rate of 20–25 percent per year, it is not surprising that prices are not stable. It would seem as if inflation is the product of the "invisible hand" operating in the *political* market: the undesirable consequence of the interplay of the actions of various groups, each pursuing its own interest and unintentionally determining an outcome that damages them all. The real culprit seems to have been the abandonment of a fiscal constitution constraining government growth. The paradox, in the case of Italy, is that such a constraint exists and it is explicit, in the form of one of the articles of Italy's written Constitution.

Inflation Forever?

> In questions of power let no more be heard of confidence in man, but bind him down from mischief by the chains of the constitution.
>
> Thomas Jefferson, 1798

The Italian Constitution

If the analysis of the previous chapter is correct, the "vicious circle of irresponsibility" is the natural, expected outcome of a system of unlimited democracy, where the government push is not constrained by a fiscal constitution. Any democracy that is caught in the delusion of believing that all that is needed to keep the growth of government under control is a freely elected Parliament will, sooner or later, be infected by the interplay of irresponsibilities described above. As Professor Buchanan has pointed out: " 'the fallacy of free elections'...presumes that governments can be and are effectively controlled so long as politicians and parties submit their records to the voters in periodic elections...if politicians 'represent' the people, the level of taxation (and public spending) cannot get seriously beyond limits desired by the citizenry at large."[1] The Italian case confirms Buchanan's view that the "fallacy of free elections" is "the most serious error ever accepted as truth by leaders of opinion." Unconstrained democratic governments do have a tendency to grow beyond the level desired by the majority of the people.

The extraordinary paradox of the Italian case is that *Italy has a fiscal constitution that was intended precisely to avoid the financial irresponsibility of government* examined. The "vicious circle of irresponsibility" is—in the case of Italy—openly unconstitutional, violating both the letter and the spirit of Italy's written Constitution, thereby providing incentive for some sober reflections on the efficacy of constitutional limitations.

The Constitution of the Republic of Italy was drafted by the Constituent Assembly, which approved it on December 22, 1947. It was then promulgated and became effective on January 1, 1948. It still is in effect. The Italian Constitution is a long, elaborate, and pretentious document, consisting of 139 articles and 18 "transitional and final arrangements." It makes delightful reading for anyone opposed to written constitutions. Its ambiguous nature and ornate prose can be easily explained by the political composition of the Constituent Assembly, a heterogeneous body of elected representatives with conflicting views about the political future of the country. Even though the members of the Constituent Assembly were highly motivated and far more qualified than contemporary parliamentarians, it can hardly be denied that they gave birth to an extraordinary collection of meaningless declarations, contradictory statements, pompous proclamations of lofty ideals devoid of content, and admirable but unenforceable provisions. The irony of the story is that one of the few areas in which the Constitution is both meaningful and enforceable — the fiscal constitution — has been gradually eroded by increasing violations that have ultimately made it ineffective.

Some articles of the Constitution are simply meaningless. It seems to me that this is true of the first paragraph of Art. 1, which states: "Italy is a democratic Republic founded on labor." No one has been able, as far as I know, to understand what "founded on labor" means. Probably, the Founding Fathers thought that it *sounded* nice. Or, take the very last article (139), that says: "The republican form is not subject to constitutional amendment." This humorously naive pretense to expropriate all future generations of their sovereignty, by denying them the right to change the republican form of government if a majority of them so pleases, can only be labeled meaningless. All that is needed to understand the meaninglessness of this "irreversible" provision is to envisage a large majority of anti-republicans passing an amendment that abrogates Art. 139, thereby making it constitutional to change the republican form.[2]

In other areas, the Constitution contradicts itself. For example, Art. 3 says in its first paragraph: "All citizens have equal social dignity and are equal before the law, without distinction of sex, of race, of language, of religion, of political opinion, of personal and social condition." Furthermore, Art. 17 guarantees the right to form associations of any kind, provided they do not violate penal laws or pursue military aims. And yet, n. XII of the "transitional and final arrangements" in its first paragraph states: "The reorganization under any form whatsoever of the dissolved Fascist party is prohibited." Still today, this provision provides matter for a debate on whether one of the parties represented in Parliament (MSI) should be outlawed because "Fascist." Clearly, Art. 3 and Art. 17 notwithstanding, some Italians are more equal than others even "before the law."

Examples of the quixotic nature of the Italian Constitution are numerous. Take, for instance, Art. 4:

The Republic recognizes the right of all citizens to work and promotes the conditions which render this right effective.

Every citizen has the duty to develop, according to his own capabilities and his own choice, an activity or function which contributes to the material or spiritual progress of society.

Here, the first paragraph can be interpreted as a commitment to full employment on the part of the republican government. It is highly questionable, however, that a full employment policy is sufficient to guarantee the protection of a "right" to work for all citizens. What is absolutely meaningless is the second paragraph: at first sight it would seem as if it states that everybody has a "duty" to work, or that society has some kind of property right in each individual's capabilities. However, when the question of who is to decide if the individual is in fact fulfilling his duty to society is asked, the reference to "his own choice" makes the entire article meaningless, a remarkable exercise in futility.

Other articles of the Constitution are simple statements of intentions, which were supposed to become effective by the enactment of *ad hoc* laws. As we have seen in the case of trade unions (Art. 39) and strikes (Art. 40), in many cases these laws have not been made, so that all that is left of the Constitution is an empty statement of intentions. These intentions have often been flagrantly violated by deliberate government policies, as in the case of Art. 47 ("The Republic encourages and protects saving in all its forms...")—savers have been regularly robbed by inflation and confiscatory taxation—and the second paragraph of the same Art. 47 ("It favors the direction of popular savings to residential property...")—an admirable intention, flagrantly contradicted by rent controls, punitive legislation, and mortgage laws that make it almost impossible to buy a house by borrowing.

These and many other examples can be cited in support of the vague and often improbable nature of a substantial portion of the Italian Constitution. They have been mentioned here as evidence of the fact that violations of the Constitution are often rooted in the excessively ambitious and/or vague nature of many of its articles. This is probably one of the main reasons behind the failure of the fiscal constitution, which, contrary to the aforementioned examples, is meaningful, enforceable, and extremely important for the survival of a free democracy. Had all the other articles been as meaningful and enforceable, had the number of general statements been kept to a minimum, had their content been clearly stated, violations of the Constitution would have been much harder to carry out and they would have been easily detected and brought to the attention of the Constitutional Court, beside being deplored by public opinion. But, when the Constitution is drafted in such a way that most of its content either does not make sense, or is by its very nature doomed to be violated, it is not surprising that even those parts of the Constitution that do make sense and that should be enforced end up being ignored and repeatedly violated. Such is the case of the fiscal constitution.

Inflation is Unconstitutional

The first, important principle of the Italian fiscal constitution is that embodied in Art. 23, contained in Part I: Rights and Duties of Citizens, Title I: Civil relations. Art. 23 may be translated as follows: "No personal or patrimonial obligation may be imposed except on the basis of law."[3]

It is worth noting that the distinction between "personal" and "patrimonial" obligations is an artificial one. The most obvious example of "personal" obligation, compulsory military draft, can be viewed as a form of discriminatory taxation in kind, thus a "patrimonial" obligation. As for the most typical "patrimonial" obligation, namely taxation, it has been acutely pointed out that it has a very "personal" dimension. Thus, Robert Nozick states:

> Taxation of earnings from labor is on a par with forced labor....taking the earnings of *n* hours of labor is like taking *n* hours from the person; it is like forcing the person to work *n* hours for another's purpose.... Seizing the results of someone's labor is equivalent to seizing hours from him and directing him to carry on various activities. If people force you to do certain work, or unrewarded work, for a certain period of time, they decide what you are to do and what purposes your work is to serve apart from your decisions. This process whereby they take this decision from you makes them a *part-owner* of you; it gives them a property right in you.[4]

The fact that the distinction is artificial, however, does not mean that the article should have been phrased differently. The form adopted might be repetitious, but it leaves no doubt that the intended meaning of the article was to declare all obligations of any kind unconstitutional, unless introduced by a formal legislative process. The *ratio legis* is obvious: given the fact that all obligations imposed on individuals infringe on the citizens' personal liberty, the protection of individual liberty requires some form of guarantee against arbitrary infringement. Such a guarantee, in a parliamentary democracy, is afforded by the formal—parliamentary—legislative process. This is the natural, physiological way to make sure that only those obligations that are essential to the survival of the state are introduced and that no unnecessary and/or arbitrary infringement on individual liberty is imposed.

Art. 23 is an admirable, meaningful, and necessary article, and one that is stated in unequivocal terms. Literally interpreted—and there is

70

no reason why it should not be so interpreted — it means that inflation is unconstitutional. As we have repeatedly said, inflation is a tax on nominal assets. As such, it is undoubtedly a "patrimonial" obligation and a rather substantial one in Italy in the past decade. Since it has not been formally legislated, therefore, inflation contradicts Art. 23 and must be regarded as unconstitutional. Such a view would, probably, be scorned and labeled naive or quixotic by many Italian constitutional scholars. Unless they resort to the improbable view, however, that inflation, like the weather, is something that falls on us unexpectedly, something which we cannot control, their view is untenable. If inflation is the result of too rapid a rate of growth of the quantity of money, economic theory suggests that enforcement of the principle of Art. 23 means that all money creation must be subject to a formal legislative process, in order to make sure that no obligation is imposed on the citizenry that is not properly legislated.

This interpretation of the article holds true even for those instances in which the creation of money is sure to be non-inflationary. Even if it does not result in inflation, money creation inevitably results in a claim on real resources on the part of the government. The absorption of these resources amounts to an obligation, and it should, therefore, be subject to parliamentary control in accordance to Art. 23. Properly interpreted, therefore, the principle of Art. 23 means that *monetary policy* should be subject to parliamentary control, and this is perfectly in line with recent developments in other countries and with established monetary policy recommendations by several economic theorists.

Unfortunately, Art. 23 is one of those articles of the Italian Constitution that have simply been *ignored*. A good example of the general attitude toward this very important principle of the Constitution is given by a recent monumental collection of essays by distinguished legal scholars devoted to the "economic" articles of the Constitution.[5] In the whole book Art. 23 is never mentioned. Even more surprising, in one of the longer essays, devoted to "the government of the economy,"[6] the author explicitly addresses the question of whether "objectively inflationary" measures are "legitimate" — that is constitutional — or not. In support of the thesis that inflationary policies are unconstitutional, articles 53, 81, and 47 are mentioned, but nowhere in the article is Art. 23 named.

Art. 47 is the improbable one mentioned above, which makes the "encouragement and protection" of savings an aim of the Republic. Obviously inflation does not recommend itself as the most appropriate way to encourage saving. Art. 53 attracts the author's attention to a greater extent than the others. It says: "All are bound to contribute to public expenses in proportion to their taxable capacity. The system of taxation conforms to the criteria of progressivity." This is the most important reason, according to the author, in favor of the unconstitutionality of inflation: it is not a progressive tax. However, the author's conclusion is that, articles 47, 53, and 81 notwithstanding, inflation is constitutionally legitimate if it is aimed at bailing out problem firms, or if it is required "in order to offset unfavorable situations in foreign trade" (sic).

According to the author, the coercive and arbitrary absorption of resources achieved through inflation should, "whenever possible," be implemented without violating "the principle of equality." We are not told what such a principle means, nor how it is possible to engage in an inflationary policy without creating arbitrary and unjustified changes in the distribution of wealth. The extensive body of empirical evidence and theoretical work on the redistributive impact of inflation is simply ignored. All that is needed in order to make a deliberate inflationary policy consistent with the principles of the Constitution is an appeal to Art. 2, which states:

> The Republic recognizes and guarantees the inviolable rights of man, whether as an individual or in social groups through which his personality develops, and requires the fulfillment of inalienable duties of political, economic, and social solidarity.

How the vague and cryptic appeal to the "inalienable duties" of "social solidarity" can be interpreted as implying that an unlegislated obligation may be imposed on the citizens, despite the letter of Art. 23 to the contrary, we are not told. It is thanks to this kind of juridical "science" that the Italian fiscal constitution has been ignored.

The Fiscal Constraint

The cornerstone of Italy's fiscal constitution is Article 81, which says:

> The Chambers approve each year the budget and the account of expenditures presented by the Government.

> Provisional exercise of the budget may not be conceded except by law and for periods which total not more than four months.

> After approval of the budget by law, new taxes and new expenditures may not be established.

> Every other law which involves new or greater expenditures must indicate the means to meet them.

Although the whole article is of great importance for the budget process in Italy, I shall concentrate on the last paragraph and its history, which are more immediately relevant for our present purposes.

The history of the introduction of the last paragraph of Art. 81 in the Italian Constitution is worth summarizing, as it leaves no doubts about the intended meaning of the principle embodied in it. On October 24, 1946, a meeting of the second sub-committee of the Constituent Assembly took place. After having debated other problems, the members of the sub-committee turned their attention to the question of whether Parliament in general, and its members in particular, should be given power of initiative in financial matters. One of the first members to express his point of view on the matter was Luigi Einaudi, a scholar of financial problems and a statesman, who, in his capacity as Governor of the Bank of Italy, succeeded in restoring monetary stability in Italy after World War II. Einaudi's position is very important, because he is generally considered to be the first and most active supporter of the last paragraph of Art. 81.[7]

Einaudi's position was very clear. He felt it was dangerous to give Parliament the power of initiative in budget matters, because, whereas in the past Parliaments would resist spending projects proposed by the government, in recent times the rule had been reversed. Popularity-seeking parliamentarians often proposed new expenditures without even bothering to consider how to finance them. Given this tendency, Einaudi concluded that only two solutions were possible: either deny parliamentarians the power to propose new expenditures, or force them to submit, together with their spending proposal, a corresponding proposal showing how to finance the new expenditure. According to Einaudi, this would have ensured a responsible approach to spending decisions.

The matter had already been considered by the members of the sub-committee because, after Einaudi's speech, the "Relatore" Mortati submitted the text of an article embodying Einaudi's proposal. The text was then criticized by one of the members (Laconi), who would have preferred to limit the power of initiative to only one of the two houses. After Laconi, it was Ezio Vanoni's turn. He strongly endorsed Einaudi's proposal, on the ground that it was opportune to obligate both Parliament and the government with a Constitutional rule that would "ensure a tendency toward a balanced budget." He went on to say that there should not be problems in the practical enforcement of the rule, that the government must always aim at balancing the budget and that Parliament must be thus "rigidly" constrained.

Ezio Vanoni's position is particularly interesting because he was a financial scholar and a supporter of national economic planning. He obviously believed that planning was impossible when spending decisions were made independently of other needs and without due consideration to the problem of how to finance them.

After Vanoni's speech, the Chairman read a new text—simpler,

73

shorter, and remarkably similar to the one that was finally adopted — which had been prepared by Mortati and Vanoni, and approved by Einaudi. The modified text was then criticized by Patricolo, who supported the view that Parliament and its members expressed the people's wishes and that it was up to government to find the way to finance the bills. Despite a few other criticisms, the article was approved with still another, minor change due to Bozzi. It is interesting to note that the whole meeting — which was not limited to this problem, but examined other constitutional issues — started at 5:45 pm and ended at 8 pm. The speed with which the sub-committee arrived at a decision concerning such an important constitutional principle can only mean one thing: there was widespread agreement among the members of the sub-committee on the desirability of such a principle.

The last paragraph of Art. 81 was then approved by the Constituent Assembly on October 17, 1947 with practically no opposition.

The meaning of the principle embodied in the last paragraph of Art. 81 is unequivocal to anyone who reads the proceedings of the sub-committee; its implications are even clearer to economists familiar with the work of Knut Wicksell, the great Swedish economist, who, as early as 1896, had recognized the need to couple spending proposals with proposals to cover the cost as a way to achieve financial responsibility.[8]

The widespread agreement on the need for a constitutional provision aimed at ensuring financial responsibility, evidenced by the sub-committee's speedy approval and by the lack of opposition in the final vote by the Constituent Assembly, was due to the circumstances of the time. Twenty years of Fascism had produced a healthy distrust toward excessive government and fostered the view that constitutional constraints were necessary. The "fallacy of free elections" — the view that democratic governments need not be constrained because they always and inevitably reflect the views of the majority of the people — as supported by Patricolo's speech at the sub-committee, was still a minority view. Furthermore, the financial mess produced by the great inflation of World War II made people very sensitive to the need for financial responsibility. Finally, the "orthodox" belief that governments should conduct their affairs in a financially responsible way, aiming at balancing their budget, was still widely held, as witnessed by the support given to the constitutional principle by people holding very different political views.

A good example of the general intellectual climate of the time is provided by the answers given by scholars and financial experts to a questionnaire that was circulated by the economic Committee in preparation of the Constitution. One of the questions was whether Parliament should be denied the power of initiative in spending matters or whether this power, if given, should be somehow limited. Most of the answers were in favor of denying Parliament such an initiative altogether, on the ground that its only function in the matter should be that of providing, or refusing to provide, the government with the tax revenue needed to finance its spending proposals. Most of the experts feared that Parliament, if given such a power, would abuse it for demagogic considerations and believed that a system of checks and balance was needed to prevent financial irresponsibility. Given such a general distrust of Parliament's capacity for self-constraint in spending matters, it is not surprising that the last paragraph of Art. 81 was so speedily approved: if anything, it was *less rigid* than most people thought necessary.[9]

Unfortunately, the general agreement on the desirability of the constitutional constraint did not ensure its smooth implementation. As early as the end of 1948, during the first year of existence of the new Constitution, doubts about the interpretation of the constitutional provision were raised, and the Chairman of the Senate decided to promote a meeting of the Chairmen and Vice-chairmen of both houses, together with the Chairmen of all legislative Committees, to find a common interpretation of the last paragraph of Art. 81 that could then be adopted by both houses. The result of the initiative was a report (Relazione Paratore-Petrilli, from the name of its two authors), that was supposed to settle any controversy regarding the interpretation of the principle.[10]

Luigi Einaudi, who in the meantime had been elected President of the Republic, thought it necessary to express his point of view on the report with a famous letter sent to the Minister of the Treasury Pella on December 13, 1948.[11] The letter is worth reading today because it summarizes very eloquently the philosophy of the constitutional principle as expressed by its author. Einaudi stresses from the beginning that it is essential to distinguish the formal legal interpretation of the article from the point of view of the substantive consequences of the interpretation. From the formal juridical point of view, said Einaudi, it would be difficult to disagree with the interpretation accepted by the report.

From the point of view of the practical implications of the interpretation adopted by the report, Einaudi doubted that it was compatible with the spirit of the constitutional principle embodied in Art. 81. The specific issue examined by Einaudi was the use to which to put increases in tax revenue. According to the report, Art. 81 had to be interpreted as meaning that, once the budget was approved, Parliament could not legislate in such a way as to *increase* the deficit over and above the amount planned by the budget. Parliament could, however, according to the report, decide to destine increases in tax revenue to new or greater expenditures. Einaudi criticizes such interpretation, maintaining that new expenditures should not be contemplated before the deficit had been *reduced* or eliminated. According to him, it was obvious that an interpretation aimed at going beyond the formal juridical letter of the article could not fail to recognize that the principle embodied in the article was the high priority given to the need to balance the budget. Indeed, he wrote, what is the meaning of a "balance" when one of the two quantities is greater than the other? (In Italian the word for budget is "bilancio," i.e. balance). Could it be doubted that, under the circumstances of the time, with the large budget deficit inherited from the war, the main goal for everybody should be that of balancing the budget, "the first condition for the economic progress of the country and the stability of the currency?"

The principle of Art. 81, according to the President, was that of preventing irresponsible spending decisions, divorced from a thorough analysis of how to finance them. It was "a very appropriately rigid law," that would be violated by an interpretation that would allow the existing deficit to remain unchanged. Otherwise, the principle would be formally respected but in fact violated, and its value would be nullified.

As long as the budget remained in deficit, the main preoccupation of Parliament should be that of cutting expenditures and increasing tax revenue in order to restore equilibrium in the budget. It is worth noting that Einaudi stresses that "it might very well be that the most effective way to increase total tax revenue is that of reducing the rates of existing taxes." A supply-sider *ante litteram*! Only after the budget was balanced, or showed a surplus, concluded Einaudi, increases in tax revenue could be utilized in a variety of ways: new expenditures (and, if so, which of the possible alternatives?), a reduction in existing taxation, or a reduction in the national debt. The letter is a very remarkable document, written in the lucid and clear prose that was typical of Italy's most elegant financial writer, and it leaves no doubt whatsoever about the meaning attached to the constitutional provision by its author.

Despite the President's letter and the interpretation of the principle accepted by the parliamentary report, the implementation of Art. 81 was not as smooth as its authors had hoped. As early as April 9, 1949, Einaudi had to resort to his presidential prerogative to send two laws back to Parliament, using the power given to the President of the Republic by Art. 74 of the Constitution, because, according to him, the two laws violated Art. 81.[12] The story did not end there: in the period preceding the political change brought about by the "center-left"—the socialist oriented government—there have been twelve cases of laws sent back to Parliament by the President of the Republic because they violated Art. 81 of the Constitution.[13]

The political change brought about by the "center-left" implied, among other things, that the opinion of those who opposed the principle of Art. 81 became prevalent. A former Governor of the Bank of Italy was quoted as saying that it was an "archaic" principle. Keynesianism became the dominant economic philosophy and the idea of a balanced budget was widely ridiculed. The old "orthodoxy" was abandoned, and it would be too long to narrate how the principle of Art. 81 was circumvented, despite the letter of the Constitution, the history of that provision, and pronouncements of the Constitutional Court.[14]

A graphic illustration of the violation of the constitutional principle and its effects on the financial responsibility of the government sector is given by the government deficit. It is worth repeating what has been said before. In 1951, during the "liberal" years (Einaudi was still President of the Republic), the deficit equaled 388 billion lire, 4 percent of GDP. It must not be forgotten that the Constitution of the Republic of Italy was only three years old and that the financial consequences of the war had not been yet eliminated. By 1961, the last year of the "liberal" era, the deficit had fallen to 357 billion, 1.5 percent of GDP. Then the "center-left" came in, and the abandonment of the "archaic" principle of Art. 81 started to produce its wonderful effects: by 1965 the deficit was 4.2 percent of GDP, 5.6 percent in 1970, 13.2 percent in 1975, 15.3 percent in 1978. As we have seen, in 1980 it has been equal to 11.6 percent, but it is still too early to say if such an "improvement" will not be more than offset in fiscal 1981, as it has repeatedly happened in the past, when reductions in the size of the deficit have proved to be only minor and short-lived deviations from the rapidly rising trend of financial irresponsibility.

"Modern" Interpretations

It might be worth at this point to look at the opinions of jurists on the compatibility of the increasing trend of financial irresponsibility with the Constitution and its provision. In what follows we shall refer to the monumental work of Valerio Onida that is widely considered as the "classic" legal analysis of the subject.[15] A good indication of the kind of legal disputes about the interpretation of Art. 81 in recent times is given by the contrast between the so-called "restrictive" and the so-called "extensive" interpretation of the constitutional principle. According to the "restrictive" interpretation, the obligation to indicate the means to meet new or greater expenditures applies only to those expenditures that are undertaken in the course of the current fiscal year, whereas expenditures that will be undertaken in future fiscal years can be legislated without bothering to indicate the means to meet them. Such an interpretation understandably leads Onida to conclude that, if accepted, it would nullify the meaning of the constitutional principle: any amount of new expenditures could be legislated without indicating how to pay for them, provided they are enacted from the next fiscal year and on. Such a contrast is worth mentioning as it illustrates how far we have gone from the original interpretation of the article given by its authors. Another good illustration is the opinion, shared by Onida (pp. 754–758), that laws that legislate new expenditures without indicating the amount of such expenditures do not violate the constitutional principle. How can the means to meet such expenditures be indicated when the amount of the expenditures is not we are not told.

The important question from our point of view is a different one: how can a constitutional article that was explicitly intended by its proponents to achieve a balanced budget be considered compatible with deficits of such staggering amounts? To this question we now turn, by looking at Onida's arguments in favor of such compatibility.

The author considers as an "extreme" interpretation of Art. 81 that according to which a balanced budget would result not from a discretionary decision of Parliament and the government but as "the automatic result of a legal mechanism" embodied in the Constitution. In particular, he intends to justify his opposition to the view that budget deficits violate the spirit of Art. 81 of the Constitution.

The author's first argument is that budget deficits in Italy have almost always been the rule, while balance and surplus have been the exception. According to his data, from 1862 (the first budget after the unification) there have been only 44 budget surpluses and 3 years of budget balance, and from this fact he concludes that it would be impossible to enforce a balanced budget provision. Little attention is given to the fact that it was exactly the need to correct such a "rule" that prompted the Constituent legislator to introduce the principle embodied in Art. 81. Furthermore, according to his own data, from 1862 to 1931 the number of budget deficits has been far smaller than surpluses and balances: 22 deficits versus 44 surpluses and 3 balances. It is only after 1931 that deficits become the rule; it is not surprising, therefore, that the 1946 Constituent legislator wanted to change what he regarded as an aberration attributable to an illiberal view of the state (Fascism) and to the war. Finally, to say that, since reality is unconstitutional, the Constitution is unrealistic is not very different from saying that, since there is crime, criminal laws are anachronistic.[16]

The second argument is simply stated: it is far from clear that a balanced budget is the optimal situation judged from the perspective of "modern financial theory." Here we have a good example of the impact of the Keynesian revolution, even though the author does not mention it explicitly. The interesting thing is that in this case we have a *legal* scholar who is so influenced by the power of an *economic* theory (which he probably knows only indirectly) that he comes to the rather unorthodox conclusion that economic theory should prevail over a Constitutional principle. If there is a contrast, that is, between an article of the Constitution and a "modern financial theory," according to this legal scholar, economic theory should prevail and make the article obsolete. As an economist, I cannot resist being flattered by the compliment paid to my profession.

The third argument is much more relevant: over which period of time should the budget be balanced? What is so unique about the (fiscal or calendar) year that the budget should be balanced annually? Wouldn't it be better to choose a wider time horizon over which to balance the budget so as to allow for an anticiclical fiscal policy? The fact is that, as the author implicitly admits, as soon as the "orthodox" idea that the budget should be balanced annually is abandoned, the removal of the constraint on government ensures that the budget is never balanced. Flexibility in the choice of the period over which the budget should be balanced sounds like a sensible idea. In practice, however, it means that budget deficits become the rule: from 1931 to this very day the public sector budget in Italy has always and with no exception been in deficit. This fact confirms the wisdom of the Constituent legislator in sticking to the "archaic" notion that the budget should be annually balanced.

Another interesting point against the view that Art. 81 is a balanced budget provision is that, according to the author, a balanced budget provision does not ensure a limitation on government spending and it is far from clear that such a limitation is desirable. Both of these observations might be true, but they have little to do with either the logic of a balanced budget provision, or the question of whether Art. 81 is in fact such a provision. The purpose of a balanced budget provision is that of achieving financial responsibility, by combining spending with taxing decisions. It is not necessarily *per se* a way to limit government spending. What a balanced budget provision does is to eliminate *irresponsible* spending decisions, but it has no effect on those spending proposals that are generally considered beneficial by voters and taxpayers. Its intended meaning is more moral than economic: it intends to achieve *responsibility* in spending. Furthermore, all of this has absolutely nothing to do with the interpretation of Art. 81. Regardless of whether a balanced budget provision reduces spending or not, regardless of whether a reduction in government spending is desirable or not, Art. 81 is there, an essential part of the Constitution of the Republic of Italy, and none of these arguments can justify its violation.

The author then moves to legal arguments. The first is that the Constitution does not explicitly mention the obligation to balance the budget, and that if it wanted to introduce such an obligation it would have made it explicit. This is undoubtedly true. It may be argued that, given the circumstances of the time of the enactment of the Constitution, balancing the budget appeared as a goal for the future, something that could not be achieved immediately because of the precarious financial situation inherited from the war. The Constituent legislator, therefore, preferred to ensure a "tendency" toward a balanced budget that in due time would have achieved that ultimate outcome. Such an interpretation is, as we have seen, supported unequivocally by the explicit intentions of the proponents of that article. It is, therefore, a bit too shrewd to rely on the lack of an explicit mention of the obligation to balance the budget in the Constitution in order to jump to the conclusion that no such constitutional provision exists.

The second legal argument is that the concept of "balance" (in Italian, "bilancio," i.e. budget) only implies a formal matching of revenue and expenditures, abidance by the laws of double entry accounting. That is undeniably true, but it is highly unlikely, to say the least, that the Constituent legislator would have thought it necessary to devote an article of the Constitution to make the standard accounting procedure compulsory.

It is the author's opinion that the Constituent Assembly's intention to achieve a "tendency" toward a balanced budget was due to the circumstances of the time, and that such a "tendency" in no way amounts to a legal obligation today. The intentions of those who introduced such a principle in the Constitution, according to the author, do not matter today. To interpret Art. 81 according to its proponents' intentions would be equivalent to saying that the Constitution reflects "a particular economic theory or political tendency," and this is unacceptable. It seems to me that the author considers unacceptable the interpretation of Art. 81 that is compatible with the views of its proponents and incompatible with the economic and political views of his own liking. Economic theory may be used to justify rejection of the interpretation of Art. 81 the author dislikes, but it may not be used to support such interpretation. We are not told why this should be the case.[17] The truth is that *any* interpretation of Art. 81 is of necessity, inevitably a politico-economic choice: if it is true that interpreting Art. 81 as a balanced budget provision implies a choice favorable to "orthodox" economics, it is equally true that denying that the meaning of the article amounts to a balanced budget provision implies a choice favorable to deficit spending philosophies. But the Constitution is not meant to be adjustable to whatever interpretation suits the political preferences of the interpreter. Article 81 was supposed to be a "very appropriately rigid law" and its meaning was unequivocally specified by those who authored and approved it. Those who did not like the principle should have supported a constitutional amendment, the repeal of Art. 81 and its replacement with its opposite, rather than trying to distort its meaning to such an incredible extent.

Two more arguments are worth mentioning. The first is that the "correct" interpretation, according to the author, is that Art. 81 has made it obligatory to consider how a given spending proposal must be financed, but it has said nothing as to the acceptable ways to finance it. Any form of financing new expenditures is, therefore, acceptable; Art. 81 only says that the choice must be made together with the spending decision. Such an interpretation would be very convincing for anyone who would ignore the intentions of the proponents of the principle and the problem it was designed to solve. The meaning of the principle, under this interpretation, would be very small indeed.

The last argument is very significant of the intellectual climate of the time this legal work was published. According to the author, the interpretation of Art. 81 must be seen in light of the need for central economic planning. (p. 816 ff.) The author's plea for not allowing politico-economic views to influence one's interpretation of the constitutional principle undoubtedly acquires a new meaning in such a context.

A Correct Interpretation

It would seem as if, judging from such an extensive legal analysis, the interpretation based on what Einaudi called the "strictly juridical" point of view could only contradict that based on the proponents' intentions, which concentrates on the "substantive consequences" of the chosen interpretation. Despite the apparent unreconcilable contrast, I believe that economic common sense suggests an interpretation that is compatible with both points of view. The key word in the last paragraph of Art. 81 is the term "means" ("must indicate the *means* to meet them"). In the Italian text the word is used as a plural (mezzi), which seems to suggest that the Constituent legislator thought that there was more than one constitutionally correct way to pay for "new or greater expenditures."

Now, there are basically four ways by which new or greater expenditures could be financed. The first is a reduction in other expenditures; this is obviously a perfectly constitutional way to pay for new expenditures, in no way it contradicts Art. 81. The second way is an increase in tax revenue simultaneously legislated to pay for the new expenditure. Few people would deny that this is another perfectly constitutional way to finance government spending. Problems arise only for the last two forms of financing government spending: genuine government borrowing *from the market*, and debt monetization, also referred to as borrowing from the Central Bank—i.e., money creation.

From what we have said so far it should be obvious that it is this last form of financing government spending that endangers the stability of the currency and the economic growth of the country, which the constitutional provision was designed to protect. It is also, as we have seen, an indirect violation of Art. 23 of the Constitution, in that it, in fact, introduces a new and arbitrary tax—inflation—without a proper legislative process. It seems obvious that what the proponents of Art. 81 and the Constituent Assembly wanted to achieve above all was monetary stability, and this is certainly endangered by recourse to money creation as a way to finance government spending. Also, from the point of view of financial responsibility it is obvious that money creation violates its basic presupposition, by allowing spending decisions to be made quite independently of the availability of financial resources to pay for them. It is the most obvious case of violation of the principle embodied in Art. 81.

What about the last way of financing government spending, genuine borrowing from the market? Here the interpretation may be controversial, because if it is true that the proponents of the last paragraph of Art. 81 wanted to achieve a balanced budget, which they considered a crucial goal of economic policy, it is also true that such a goal is nowhere explicitly mentioned in the Constitution. The reason for the lack of such an explicit mention might be the one suggested above, namely that at the time of the enactment of the Constitution it was believed that is was not possible to achieve it immediately. However, even the proponents of the constitutional principle recognized that there can be "exceptional circumstances"—e.g. a war—which would make a balanced budget impossible to achieve in a relatively short period of time. This is why they preferred to introduce a provision that would "ensure a tendency toward a balanced budget" rather than making an explicit reference to a (compulsory) balanced budget. It probably was a mistake on their part not to choose a more inflexible formulation of the constitutional principle, as the sad history of the Italian government deficit confirms, but it can be argued that they did not want to make such a formulation inflexible in order to make room for unforeseeable exceptional circumstances. And it would be hard to deny that the explosion of the public deficit in Italy has violated both the "tendency" toward a balanced budget and any reasonable interpretation of Art. 81.

Maybe all that was needed in order to make Art. 81 both flexible and easier to violate was a specification, an explicit indication of the constitutionally acceptable and unacceptable "means to meet" new expenditures. By stating that new expenditures could be financed only by a reduction of other expenditures or an increase in tax revenue, or "under extraordinary circumstances" by genuine borrowing *from the market*, and that they could not be financed by borrowing from the Central Bank (money creation), the Constituent legislator would have made it impossible to circumvent the constitutional principle. Constitutionally unacceptable financing would have amounted to an *open violation* of the Constitution. It is far from clear that this would have amounted to a "rigorous and effective" constraint on the growth of government and on the explosion of financial irresponsibility. The "climate of the times" has undoubtedly changed from the time of the drafting of the Constitution. At that time a surplus in the budget was considered a desirable situation. Today, the sums that the public sector fails to spend are referred to as "passive residuals" (residui passivi) and considered a "problem" to be solved quickly by increased spending. However, a constitutional provision that could only be either respected or *openly* violated would have provided a much more effective deterrent to irresponsible spending decisions. It is not entirely unreasonable to suppose that had the agreement on the need for the constitutional provision been less general, had the discussion at the sub-committee lasted a bit longer with a more qualified presence of those who opposed the constitutional principle, this would have been better phrased and expressed in a more detailed way. But for the proponents of the article it was inconceivable to think that some day there would be a majority of politicians that would openly advocate a budget deficit as a way to achieve economic prosperity. They would have, quite correctly, reregarded such a view as financially irresponsible, a sure recipe for economic disaster. Unfortunately, history has vindicated their old-fashioned, "archaic" orthodoxy; supporters of "modern financial theory" should feel ashamed of the unintended results of their "enlightened" policy prescriptions.

4

Summary and Conclusion

The question "can inflation be stopped?" has led us to examine, in the preceding pages, three related sets of problems. The first was the obvious one of what causes inflation. In the first chapter we have seen that monetary theory provides us with an unambiguous answer to that question: "inflation is always and everywhere a monetary phenomenon." There has never been a case of inflation without a previous excessive growth in the quantity of money, and there has never been rapid monetary growth without a resulting inflation. No proposition in economic theory has been empirically tested as much as that which states that inflation finds its origin in a rate of monetary growth in excess of the rate of growth of real output. Available evidence indicates that the "quantity theory of money" has passed the test, that it has failed to be falsified by empirical evidence.[1]

Despite the notoriety of the monetary theory of inflation and the impressive amount of empirical evidence in its favor, I have thought it necessary to include a brief and simplified summary of it because of the popularity of so many fallacious views on the matter. It has been shown that these alleged "causes" of inflation are neither sufficient nor necessary conditions for it.

It has also been stressed that excessive monetary growth was a *proximate* cause of inflation, meaning that increases in the quantity of money were the consequence of other factors. This has led us to our second question "what causes excessive monetary growth?" The answer to this question is provided by that branch of economic theory that I would call "politonomy" — the economic analysis of politics — also known as the "public choice" theory. In the second chapter, we have seen that politonomy suggests that the structure of incentives in unconstrained mass democracies is biased in favor of government growth. We have seen this to be true for the protagonists of democratic life: the voter, the politician, the taxpayer, businessmen and labor leaders. (A great deal could have been said about the role of the bureaucracy in the growth of government, but that has been left out for idiosyncratic considerations.) Using the Italian case as an example, we have seen how government growth translates itself into a formidable factor favoring excessive monetary growth and inflation: the government push.

The third obvious question was "how can inflationary government be constrained?" This has led us to still a third field of social analysis: constitutional engineering, and we have examined the failure of Italy's fiscal constitution to achieve financial responsibility. What lesson can be derived from what has been said?

The obvious lesson seems to be that constitutional engineering is required, in the sense that the long run inflationary bias of mass democracy requires a set of constitutional constraints aimed at enforcing financial responsibility and taming government growth. In other words, a fiscal constitution is a necessary condition for preventing increasing inflation from becoming a permanent feature of our societies.

At this point it is necessary to modify something that has been said so far. We have seen that government deficits in Italy are of such staggering proportions that it would be impossible to finance them without resorting to money creation. However, this is true of Italy but, as we have said, it is not (yet) true of other Western countries. The size of these countries' deficits relative to national income is such that it would be entirely possible to finance them without printing money. And yet, even these countries suffer from too rapid monetary growth and are plagued by inflation. Our previous emphasis on the need for a *fiscal* constitution, aimed at achieving financial responsibility in budget matters, must therefore be modified in the sense that we also need a *monetary* constitution, aimed at achieving responsibility in the conduct of monetary policy.[2] In other words, since it is possible to have inflationary monetary policy *before* financial irresponsibility makes it unavoidable, the set of constraints on inflationary government should not be limited to reducing the size of the budget deficit but should also aim at achieving a stable and predictable rate of growth of the money supply, consistent with price stability.

The obvious problem here is that it is a lot easier to agree on the *need for* a monetary-fiscal constitution than on the *kind of* constitutional constraints to adopt. In a sense even those who oppose the introduction of additional constraints agree on the need for a monetary-fiscal constitution: they are convinced that free elections are all that is needed in order to attain monetary and financial responsibility on the part of the government. Their case has never been weaker, as evidenced by the monetary instability plaguing the Western world, the reasons for which I have tried to analyze thus far.

Just to mention a few of the points of disagreement regarding the kind of constitutional framework to choose, let us look at some of the proposals that have been made in recent times. The most important, and in a sense the most appealing, of the proposals is that which would introduce *spending ceilings* on government, tying government spending to national income in a fixed predetermined ratio. Government spending would not be allowed to exceed a given percentage of GNP and its rate of growth should not exceed the rate of growth of national income. This is an admirable proposal that has been criticized, however, on two grounds. First, it is suggested that in such a way economic growth would "benefit" government by allowing public spending to grow in the same proportion. Second, a total government spending ceiling would probably end up sacrificing more heavily those categories of expenditures that benefit society as a whole (e.g., defense) than those special interest pieces of legislation that can always rely on strong lobbies in their favor.

Another popular kind of constraint is that which would establish *tax ceilings*, or aim at achieving tax cuts. It can be argued, however, that tax ceilings unaccompanied by some kind of balanced budget provision might result — as the Italian experience suggests — in an increase in "hidden" taxes, i.e., in the budget deficit. What matters most is not how we pay for government, whether in the form of explicit taxes or in the form of a deficit, but how much we have to pay.

Finally, even *balanced budget* provisions have been criticized by supporters of other kinds of constraints on the ground that they would have to leave room for "emergency situations," and this, in turn, might nullify their effectiveness.

These arguments on the relative desirability of the different proposals show that agreement on the need for a fiscal-monetary constitution is only a first step in the right direction: it is a necessary but by no means a sufficient condition for achieving a constitutional framework designed to constrain government growth.

What can be learned from the Italian experience in this regard? Let me stress once again that Italy is not a Latin American country: Italian monetary history confirms, as we have seen, that inflation has been the exception rather than the rule in Italian history. The lira has traditionally been one of the most stable currencies in Europe. The past nine years of double-digit inflation are unprecedented in the peacetime history of the country. This makes the Italian "great inflation" of the 1970s all the more remarkable and worth studying. What makes it even more interesting is the fact that available figures confirm beyond any reasonable doubt that: (a) inflation in Italy is a monetary phenomenon (the quantity theory of money works in its most simplistic form in explaining the Italian inflation of the 1970s); (b) excessive monetary growth is the consequence of the "government push" (given the size of the deficit, there is no alternative to money creation); and

(c) if the "vicious circle of irresponsibility" is not reversed (and it is doubtful that it can at this point), Italy is heading toward runaway inflation.

As we have seen, the fascinating aspect of Italy's financial troubles is that she has an admirable fiscal constitution. The Founding Fathers of the Republic of Italy correctly perceived the need for a set of constitutional constraints on government and introduced two constitutional principles that, *if interpreted correctly*, would have ensured precisely the kind of monetary-fiscal framework many people advocate today. However, to say the least, the Constitution has not been enforced. Why?

I believe that the failed enforcement of Italy's fiscal constitution is due to three sets of reasons. First of all, the general nature of the Italian Constitution, ambiguous and often quixotic and unenforceable, has weakened the chances of effectiveness even of those articles that are meaningful, important, and enforceable, such as articles 23 and 81.

Second, it can be argued that the two constitutional principles embodied in Art. 23 and in the last paragraph of Art. 81 could have been (and should have been) expressed in a more detailed way. Since they were not adequately specified, violations of the constitutional principles were not as evident as they could have been. The very peculiar interpretations of Art. 81 provide good evidence that part of the blame lies with the phrasing of the Article that is not sufficiently binding.

Finally, the change in the intellectual climate from the time of the drafting of the Constitution, the advent of the Keynesian revolution and of the deficit spending mythology proved to be an irresistible force toward a distorted interpretation of the constitutional principles.

What kind of constitutional changes would be required to restore financial responsibility and monetary stability? In my opinion, only three changes are needed, but they are not minor. First, the tax structure must be changed in order to make taxes more "visible". In order to achieve this result, tax withholding should be abolished, both for the income and for the social security taxes (the employer would turn the sums that he now pays to the taxman to the employee, who, in turn, would pay the taxman); indirect taxation (excise, sales, value added taxes) should gradually be replaced by direct taxation; and the "hidden" tax of the budget deficit should be eliminated. It is a safe bet, as we have said, that if Italians were aware of the fact that they are being coerced to give over one half of their income to the taxman, not only they would stop asking for more government and voting for statist parties, they would also stage a tax rebellion of unprecedented extent.

But this is not the main reason for making taxes visible. The fact is that the visibility of taxes is an essential component of a democratic government. In a democracy, people must be aware of the cost of government, because *they* (and no one else) bear that cost. Government of the people means, among other things, that people must control their government. This is impossible when the cost of government is hidden behind a complex cobweb of invisible taxes, understood only by those who possess the kind of sophisticated knowledge required to see through. The decision of how much government to have, of what percentage of personal income should be turned over to the government (and what percentage should be left to the free choice of the individual), in a democracy naturally belongs to the people. A political system in which government surreptitiously takes one half of their income from the people, knowing that, if they were aware of it, they would not allow it to happen, is not only a fraudulent one, it is also an undemocratic one, because it violates the people's sovereignty.

Second, a constitutional law is required to interpret Art. 23 as meaning that money creation—which undoubtedly represents a "patrimonial obligation"—should be subject to the control of Parliament, in the sense that at the beginning of the legislature the Central Bank would submit the target rate(s) of growth of the money supply for the whole legislature (five years) to Parliament. These would be enacted through a formal legislative procedure, and Parliament would be in charge of making sure that they are regularly attained. Such a system would not, of course, ensure that the chosen rate of monetary growth is the "right" one. The chosen rate might prove to be too high or too low. But this change would accomplish two things: it would eliminate the kind of instability produced by the variability of the rate of monetary growth over time (because the chosen rate could not be changed for five years), and it would eliminate the kind of surreptious expropriation of resources produced by money creation. Under such a system, at least, money creation would result not from the whims of "independent" central bankers but from a procedure controlled by Parliament. This, in my opinion, is the most that can be hoped for in the way of a monetary constitution.

Finally, another constitutional law should interpret the meaning of the last paragraph of Art. 81, eliminating the existing ambiguity and the uncertainties regarding that meaning. The desirable interpretation should indicate that the only acceptable "means" to meet new or greater expenditures are: (a) reductions in other expenditures, (b) *ad hoc* increases in explicit taxes, and (c) under "emergency conditions" government borrowing *from the market*. This would make debt monetization illegal and put an end to the financing of the deficit achieved through printing money.

Needless to say, the chances of such changes being introduced in Italy are only marginally different from zero. And this is tragic, because Italy, like no other country, today confirms that one can have only two of the following three: democracy, monetary stability, unconstrained government. Today, we have democracy and unconstrained government, but no monetary stability. If inflation accelerates, we might be forced to choose between constraining government or having to give up democracy. Believers in democracy have one duty above all today: if they want to preserve a free and democratic society, they must support the introduction of effective constraints on government.

The Italian experience should teach other countries that a monetary-fiscal constitution is necessary. Indeed, if one agrees that the "Italian disease" is only a more acute form of the same disease that affects all Western societies, the need for a set of constraints on inflationary government is an urgent one. It is the most that other countries can do in order to avoid falling into the kind of financial disarray that is currently plaguing Italy.

But the Italian experience also teaches another, less optimistic, lesson: although monetary-fiscal constitutions are necessary, they are far from being a sufficient guarantee against excessive government. There is no such a thing as a foolproof legal device that can protect our freedom forever. There is no substitute for our constant alertness, for our awareness of the threat posed to our freedom by an ever-growing leviathan.

Footnotes

Chapter 1

1. This has not always been the case. Not long ago, leading economists — mostly in the Keynesian tradition — were denying that inflation had any substantial negative impact on social welfare. For example, *see* James Tobin, "Inflation and Unemployment," *American Economic Review*, March 1972.

2. Milton Friedman, "Inflation: Causes and Consequences," in *Dollars and Deficits*, Prentice-Hall, 1968, p. 39.

3. On the falsification principle, *see* Karl Popper, *The Logic of Scientific Discovery*, Hutchinson & Co., 1974, chs. III and IV.

4. *See,* for example, Harry G. Johnson, *Essays in Monetary Economics*, Harvard University Press, 1967, p. 104; Milton Friedman, *Dollars and Deficits*, Prentice-Hall Inc., 1968, p. 21; Robert M. Solow, "Learning the Lessons of Inflation," *Economic Impact*, n. 3, 1976.

5. It must be noted that Q does not necessarily coincide with real income produced, if there are changes in inventories. Society can purchase more than is produced — even if we assume a closed economy — if inventories are reduced, and it can purchase less than is produced if inventories are increased. To avoid this complication, let's assume that inventories are stable (equilibrium level) so that, in our closed economy, Q coincides with real income produced in that particular time period. The price level then becomes the ratio of what society spends to what society produces.

6. This view does not necessarily contradict the notion that the Keynesian theory and the quantity theory of money are special cases of a more general theory. The fact is that as "engines for the discovery of concrete truths" the two necessarily compete.

7. For an example of an early test of the relative validity of the two models, *see* Milton Friedman and David Meiselman, "The Relative Stability of Monetary Velocity and the Investment Multiplier in the United States, 1897–1958," *CMC*, Prentice-Hall Inc., 1963, pp. 165–268.

8. "There has never been a sustained inflation of prices that has not been financed by an increase in the quantity of money. To admit this, one does not have to be a monetarist or a quantity theorist in every respect. One merely has to realize that the amount of inactive cash balances is limited." Fritz Machlup, "Different Inflations Have Different Effects on Employment," *Banca Nazionale del Lavoro Quarterly Review*, n. 127, December 1978, p. 292.

9. Peter Wiles, "The New Inflation Consists of Too Many Bankers Chasing Too Few Ideas," in *Anti-inflationary Policies: East–West*, Ceses, Quaderni n.6, 1975, p. 238.

10. A. A. Alchian & W. R. Allen, *University Economics*, Belmont, 1964, pp. 106–107.

11. This fundamental difference in approach reflects the difference between "P-economists" and "Q-economists," to use a definition coined by Sir John R. Hicks. *See*, "Methods of Dynamic Analysis," in *25 Essays in Honour of E. Lindhal*, Stockholm, 1956, pp. 139 ff. The economists of the "P" type (the monetarists, in our case) tend to assume quantities as given, at least in the short run, and analyze short-run adjustments in terms of price variations. The "Q-economists," on the other hand, assume prices to be given, and explain short run adjustments in terms of variations of quantities. At the macro-level, the difference stems from the fact that the macroeconomic model common to both Keynesian and monetary economists is undetermined: the number of equations is less than the number of unknowns. Therefore, monetary economists assume "exogenous" (constant) real income and its rate of growth, and employ the model to determine the price level (and the rate of inflation). Keynesians, on the other hand, assume constant prices and proceed in determining the equilibrium value of real income (and its rate of growth). For a classic summary of the controversy in the interpretation here accepted, *see* Milton Friedman, "A Theoretical Framework for Monetary Analysis," *Journal of Political Economy*, March 1970, pp. 193 ff.

12. C. Bresciani-Turroni, *The Economics of Inflation — A Study of Currency Depreciation in Post-war Germany, 1914–1923*, London, 1937.

13. *The Economic Journal*, XLVIII, September 1938, pp. 507–513.

14. This point is misunderstood by the non-monetarists. Thus, for example, Lord Kahn comes out with the proposition: "It can be readily conceded to the monetarists that an increase in the quantity of money, though not the *cause* of inflation, is necessary condition." ("Thoughts on the Behavior of Wages and Monetarism," *Lloyd's Bank Review*, January 1976, p. 6). Now, to say that an increase in the quantity of money is a necessary condition of inflation is equivalent to saying that inflation is necessarily a monetary phenomenon. On Lord Kahn's own admission, if the quantity of money is kept under control there can be no inflation. The difference between a "cause" and a "necessary condition" is meaningless from the point of view of monetary analysis, at least in this respect.

15. C. Bresciani-Turroni, *op. cit.*, p. 23.

16. *Ibid.*, p. 156.

17. *Ibid.*

18. *Ibid.*

19. *Ibid.*, p. 82.

20. Milton Friedman, "Money: Quantity Theory," *International Encyclopedia of the Social Sciences*, Macmillan Co. and the Free Press, 1968, Vol. 10, p. 442.

21. Martin Bailey, *National Income and the Price Level*, McGraw-Hill, 1962, pp. 53–54.

22. Milton Friedman, *Milton Friedman in Australia 1975*, The Clarendon Press, Kensington, 1975, p. 10.

23. "...[G]rasping trade unions...may by their actions steadily raise the minimum money value of the full-employment income and so make stable prices and full-employment incompatible...." Milton Friedman, "The Effects of a Full-Employment Policy on Economic Stability: A Formal Analysis," in *Essays in Positive Economics*, Chicago, 1953, p. 120.

24. "Unless the cost-push produces a monetary expansion that would otherwise not have occurred, its effect will be limited to at most a temporary general price rise accompanied by unemployment...." Milton Friedman, "What Price Guidepost?", in *Guidelines, Informal Controls, and the Marketplace*, Chicago, 1966, p. 21.

25. Tom Wilson, "The Impact of Inflation and Economic Growth," in *The Dilemmas of Government Expenditure*, I.E.A., London, 1976, pp. 32–33.

26. *See also* Gottfried Haberler, "Wage-Push Inflation Once More," in *Roads to Freedom, Essays in Honor of F. A. von Hayek*, London, 1969, p. 66: "...modern collective bargaining by powerful labor organizations confronts the monetary authorities with the disagreeable dilemma either to permit enough inflation to maintain full employment at the higher, union-imposed money wages, or to keep prices stable at the expense of a certain amount of unemployment."

27. Of the extensive bibliography on the subject, *see* Milton Friedman, *Inflation and Unemployment: The New Dimension of Politics*, I.E.A., London, 1977.

   "...[T]he implication of the Phillips Curve...is that at the price of a higher rate of price inflation a larger reduction of unemployment can be achieved. The experience of the last ten years has contradicted this presumption. In many countries both the rate of price inflation and the rate of unemployment have increased. Some economists have expressed their disappointment about the 'strange' way in which the economy was behaving; they spoke of a 'new type' of inflation, never observed before, and not yet understood by them or their colleagues. What seems strange to me is that these disappointed economists regard as new, unexpected, and unexplained a phenomenon which other economists had described, explained, and predicted. Many things seem new to those who do not read." Fritz Machlup, "Different Inflations Have Different Effects on Employment," *op. cit.*, p. 301.

   Also, in a polemic with James Tobin, Gordon Tullock has pointed out that the very idea of the Phillips Curve is based on the delusion that one can "fool all the people all the time." See Gordon Tullock, "Can You Fool All the People All the Time," *Journal of Money, Credit, and Banking*, May 1972, pp. 426–430; James Tobin & L. Ross, "A Reply to Gordon Tullock," *ibid.*, pp. 431–436; G. Tullock "Inflation and Unemployment: the Discussion Continued," *Journal of Money, Credit, and Banking*,

August 1973, pp. 826–835; J. Tobin, "More on Inflation," *Journal of Money, Credit, and Banking*, November 1973, pp. 982–984.

F. A. Hayek has pointed out that the Phillips Curve might very well be positively sloped – in that inflation might result in an *increase* of unemployment because of the distortion in the structure of relative prices. See F. A. Hayek, *Full Employment at Any Price?*, I.E.A., London, 1975.

Lately, there seems to be widespread agreement that there is no such a thing as a trade-off between inflation and unemployment. *See*, for example, T. D. Willett and L. O. Laney, "Monetarism, Budget Deficits, and Wage Push Inflation: The Cases of Italy and the U.K.," *Banca Nazionale del Lavoro Quarterly Review*, December 1978: "A further complication is that we cannot be sure that a policy of consistently validating inflationary shocks would minimize unemployment even if we decided that this was the most important objective. Higher rates of inflation tend to be associated with greater economic and financial uncertainty, which can in turn generate higher levels of unemployment over the medium term." p. 319.

28. C. Rowley, "Buying Out the Obstructors?" in S. C. Littlechild *et al., The Taming of Government*, Readings 21, I.E.A., London, 1979, pp. 107–118.

29. R. E. Wagner and R. D. Tollison, *Balanced Budgets, Fiscal Responsibility, and the Constitution*, Cato Institute, 1980, pp. 9–10.

30. Patrick Minford, "Monetarism, Inflation and Economic Policy," in *Is Monetarism Enough?* I.E.A., London, 1980, pp. 3–23.

31. A similar argument has been put forth by Michael Beenstock in the discussion on Minford's paper, *op. cit.*, p. 24.

32. This seems to be even Minford's own conclusion: "I confirm...(the)... interpretation of my argument that a rise in the ...(government deficit)...leads over some time-scale to complementary rises in monetary growth." p. 30.

33. These are the percentages quoted by Minford in the paper mentioned above. *See op. cit.*, p. 7, Table 1.

34. For a classic full analysis of the exchange rate controversy, *see* Milton Friedman, "The Case for Flexible Exchange Rates" in *Essays in Positive Economics*, University of Chicago Press, Chicago, 1953.

35. Gottfried Haberler, "The Dollar in the World Economy: Recent Developments in Perspective," in American Enterprise Institute, *Contemporary Economic Problems 1980,* p. 140.

36. *Ibid.*, pp. 161–162.

37. This seems to be confirmed by empirical research, at least for the United Kingdom and Italy: "...our empirical results suggest that the high rates of monetary expansion and inflation in these two countries have been largely home-grown rather than imported." T. D. Willett and L. O Laney, *op. cit.*, pp. 316–317.

38. *Milton Friedman in Australia 1975, op. cit.*, pp. 35–36. Also, "Monetary growth, like inflation, can and does vary over a much wider range than output growth. Doubling the trend rate of output growth in a few years would be phenomenal, yet for the UK, that would reduce inflation by only

two or three percentage points." M. Friedman, "Response to Question-naire on Monetary Policy," *Appendices to the minutes of evidence taken before the Treasury and Civil Service Committee*, London, June 1980, p. 55.

Chapter 2

1. M. Friedman, "Response to Questionnaire on Monetary Policy," *op. cit.*, p. 59.

2. The fact that the time pattern of the inflation rate mirrors monetary changes, even disregarding output changes, seems to suggest that mone-tary policy in Italy in the 1970s has had no effect on output—the whole impact being on prices. This is not peculiar to Italy: "there seems little if any relation between monetary change and output: a simple quantity the-ory that regards price change as determined primarily by monetary change and output by independent other factors fits the evidence for the period as a whole (excluding wars)... The whole of a change in the quantity of money is absorbed sooner or later by prices...." M. Friedman, "Re-sponse...," *op. cit.*, p. 60.

3. F. Machlup, "Different Inflations," *op. cit.*

4. The PSBR/GNP ratio in the UK is that given by R. Dornbusch in his re-sponse to the "Questionnaire on Monetary Policy," *op. cit.*, p. 69. His conclusion that "empirically, both in the US and the UK, there appears no stable relationship between deficits and money creation" is undoubtedly valid for those two countries, where the PSBR/GNP ratio is much smaller than in Italy. As we shall see, however, it would be impossible to borrow 12 percent of GNP from the market in order to finance the deficit in a non-inflationary way.

5. *Relazione Annuale*, May 31, 1979. Another effect of the rapid increase in government spending is the absorption of private savings. The percentage of private household savings going to the public sector has increased from 29 percent in 1969 to 62 percent in 1973. See *Relazione Annuale*, May 31, 1974.

6. See *Tendenze Monetarie*, n. 34, July 2, 1979.

7. T. D. Willett and L. O. Laney, *op. cit.*, p. 323. This is also M. Parkin's view: "Given the way in which monetary policy is conducted in Britain,... there is a remarkable, though of course not precise, link between the pub-lic sector borrowing requirement and monetary expansion. In principle, it is possible to finance the public sector's deficit without creating money, provided interest rates are allowed to rise to high enough levels. However, because of preoccupation with the cost of borrowing, particularly in the housing sector, such interest rate movements are not typically permitted, with the result that variations in the over-all borrowing requirement lead directly to variations in the rate of monetary expansion." *See* Michael Parkin, "Where is Britain's Inflation Going?" *Lloyd's Bank Review*, July 1975, p. 11.

As an alternative to monetary growth, ceilings on maximum interest rates have at times been suggested. It can be shown, however, that the attempt to legislate a reduction on interest rates below their market level may, under certain assumptions, lead to runaway inflation. *See* Antonio Martino, "Inflationary Finance and 'the' Interest Rate," *Rivista di Politica Economica, Selected Papers*, n. 11, 1977, pp. 79–92.

8. M. Friedman, "The Fed and Inflation," *Newsweek*, December 29, 1980.

9. R. E. Wagner and R. D. Tollison, *Balanced Budgets, Fiscal Responsibility, and the Constitution, op. cit.*, p. 11.

10. M. Friedman, "Response...," *op. cit.*, p. 55–56. Professor Friedman's view, however, should not be interpreted as meaning that money creation is of necessity the only way to finance the deficit. "...wartime periods aside, many other factors typically affect the rate of monetary growth, so that there is only the loosest relation in practice between monetary growth and deficits." M. Friedman, "Deficits and Inflation," *Newsweek*, February 22, 1981, p. 70.

11. In the words of the then Governor of the Bank of Italy:

> We have asked, and still ask ourselves the question if the Bank of Italy could have refused or could still refuse to finance the deficit of the public sector by refraining from using the faculty given by the law to buy State securities. The refusal would make it impossible for the State to pay salaries to the public members of the military order, of the judiciary order, of the civil order, and pensions to citizens in general. It would look like an act of monetary policy; but would in fact be a seditious act, that would be followed by the paralysis of the institutions. (my translation)

See Relazione del governatore della Banca d'Italia sull'esercizio 1973, Considerazioni finali, Banca d'Italia, Roma, 1974, p. 30.

12. M. Parkin, "Where is Britain's Inflation Going?", *op. cit.*, p. 3.

13. Franco Reviglio, *Il significato economico della rivalutazione dei conti nazionali, op. cit.*

14. The estimate for 1980 is the official one: see *Relazione sul fabbisogno del settore pubblico*, presented to Parliament by the Minister of the Treasury, F. M. Pandolfi, in April 1980.

15. *Einaudi Notizie*, 1980, p. 12.

16. For an excellent recent work on the subject, see James T. Bennett and Manuel H. Johnson, *The Political Economy of Federal Government Growth: 1959–1978*, Center for Education and Research in Free Enterprise, Texas A & M University, 1980.

17. Sir Karl Popper considers the conspiracy theory of society as "more primitive than most forms of theism" and "akin to Homer's theory of society." "Homer conceived the power of the gods in such a way that whatever happened on the plain before Troy was only a reflection of the various conspiracies on Olympus. The conspiracy theory of society is just a version of this theism, of a belief in gods whose whims and wills rule everything." (*Conjectures and Refutations*, London, 1963, p. 123). Obviously, if one is convinced that all social evils are the intended result of the actions of wicked

men, one does not need any explanation of the various problems. All that is needed is to find the culprit and make sure he receives the appropriate punishment. Unfortunately, things are never so simple. No one *planned* the growth of government and the resulting inflation. We still need, therefore, an explanation of the phenomenon.

18. D. Friedman, *The Machinery of Freedom*, 1973, p. 146.

19. A good example of negative sum game statism: "Between 1960 and 1974, the total level of expenditure on social welfare programs in the United States increased $120 billion, from $50 billion to $170 billion. According to the Bureau of Census there are 25 million poor people in the United States, defined as people with an income level of $4,137 or less for a given year for a family of four. If that $120 billion — not the whole budget, just the increase — had simply been given to the poor, it would have given each and every one of them an annual stipend of $4,800 a year, or $19,200 for every family of four." (Arianna Stassinopoulos, "The Inflation of Politics and the Disintegration of Culture," *Imprimis*, March 1978).

20. For a full discussion of this particular asymmetry, see James M. Buchanan and Richard E. Wagner, "Democracy and Keynesian Constitutions: Political Biases and Economic Consequences," in *The Consequences of Mr. Keynes*, Hobart Paper 78, I.E.A., London, 1978, pp. 11–27, especially pp. 18–23.

21. "The widespread enthusiasm for reducing government taxes and other impositions is not matched by a comparable enthusiasm for eliminating government programs — except programs that benefit other people," Milton Friedman and Rose D. Friedman, *Free to Choose: A Personal Statement*, Harcourt Brace Jovanovich, Inc., 1980.

22. Such is unfortunately the case of Italy. Article 75 of the Italian Constitution states:

> Article 75. Popular *referendum* is established to determine the abrogation, total or partial, of a law, or of an act having the force of law, when it is demanded by 500,000 electors or by five regional Councils.
> The *referendum* is not permitted for tax laws or laws on the budget, for laws of amnesty and of pardon, or for laws authorizing the ratification of international treaties."

Therefore, taxpayers' resistance in Italy lacks the legal possibility of resorting to a popular referendum.

23. For the figures on fiscal pressure, see Istituto Centrale di Statistica, *I Conti degli Italiani*, Roma, 1979. Explicit taxes have increased very rapidly, from 28 percent in 1958 to 38.4 percent in 1978. *See I Conti degli Italiani*, Roma, 1974, p. 62.

24. Richard Rose, "The Makings of a Do-It-Yourself Tax Revolt," *Public Opinion*, Aug./Sept. 1980. For the underground economy in Italy, see A. Martino, "Measuring Italy's Underground Economy," *Policy Review*, n. 16, Spring 1981.

25. I have not mentioned the pressures in favor of government growth that come from the bureaucracy, because I am convinced that in Italy they are

minor compared to those of voters and politicians. They would, however, only strengthen the argument. For an analysis of such a problem, see Gordon Tullock, *The Politics of Bureaucracy*, Public Affairs Press, Washington, D.C., 1965; and W. A. Niskanen, *Bureaucracy and Representative Government*, Chicago, 1971.

26. V. Pareto, *Cours d'économie politique*, 1896. In *Sociological Writings*. Translated by Derick Mirfin and edited by S. E. Finer. London: Pall Mall Press, 1966, as quoted in *The Year of Economists 1980–81*, compiled by George J. Stigler and Claire Friedland, Chicago: University of Chicago Press, 1980.

27. J. M. Buchanan, "The Limits of Taxation," paper presented at the Mont Pelerin Society Meeting, Hoover Institution, Stanford, California, September 1980, p. 6.

28. G. Salvemini, *Under the Axe of Fascism*, 1936, p. 416. For a contemporary "rediscovery" of the economic policy of Fascism, presented as a "new" formula, *see* William Greider, "The Conservative Way to American Socialism," *The Washington Post*, September 14, 1980.

29. John Burton, "Trade Unions' Role in the British Disease: 'An Interest in Inflation'?," in *Is Monetarism Enough?*, I.E.A., London, 1980, pp. 99 ff.

30. The average annual increase in hourly earnings in manufacturing from 1965 to 1977 has been 15.2 percent in Italy, as compared to 12.2 percent in France, 12.1 percent in Belgium, 12 percent in the United Kingdom, 10.9 percent in Holland, and 8.4 percent in West Germany. See *The Economist*, February 25, 1978.

31. Article 39 of the Italian Constitution says:

The organization of trade unions is free. No other obligation may be imposed on a trade union except that of registering at local or central public offices, in accordance with the norms established by law. A condition for registration is that the statutes of the unions sanction an internal organization on a democratic basis. Registered trade unions have legal personality. They may, being represented as units in proportion to their membership stipulate collective labor contracts with obligatory efficacy for all those members of the category of labor to which the contract refers.

Since the law that was supposed to enact this article has never been passed, labor unions do not have to register and, since they do not legally exist, they operate outside the law, being as it were *legibus soluti*. Article 40 says: "The right to strike is exercised within the sphere of the laws which regulate it." Again, these laws do not exist, so that all that is left of the constitutional principle is an unlimited and unregulated right to strike, that the unions use wildly — as the figures in Table 6 suggest. The above translation of the two articles is that of N. Kogan, *The Government of Italy*, New York, 1962, p. 194.

32. J. Hicks, *The Crisis in Keynesian Economics*, Oxford, 1974, p. 61.

33. J. M. Keynes, *The General Theory of Employment, Interest, and Money*, (1936) New York: Harcourt, Brace and World, Inc. 1964, p. 14.

34. J. M. Keynes, "Borrowing for Defense: Is it Inflation?," *The Times*, 11 March, 1937, reprinted in T. W. Hutchinson, *Keynes v. the 'Keyne-*

sians'. . .? *An Essay in the Thinking of J. M. Keynes and the Accuracy of its Interpretation by his Followers*, I.E.A., London, 1977.

35. J. M. Buchanan and R. E. Wagner, "Democracy and Keynesian Constitutions: Political Biases and Economic Consequences," in J. M. Buchanan, J. Burton, R. E. Wagner, *The Consequences of Mr. Keynes*, I.E.A., London, 1978, p. 15.

36. T. Wilson, "The Impact of Inflation and Economic Growth," *op. cit.*, p. 36.

37. J. M. Buchanan and R. E. Wagner, *op. cit.*

38. Giuseppe de Meo, *Aspetti Statistici dell'Inflazione*, Annali di Statistica, Serie VIII, Vol. 30, Istituto Centrale di Statistica, Roma, 1980, pp. 66–67.

39. T. D. Willett and L. O. Laney, "Monetarism, Budget Deficits. . .," *op. cit.*, p. 331, footnote.

40. *See* J. T. Bennett and M. H. Johnson, *The Political Economy of Federal Government Growth: 1959–1978*, *op. cit.*, pp. 76–80, and the bibliography therein.

41. "Inflation and Its Causes in a 'Mixed' Economy: the Italian Case," in *Scritti Monetari*, La Cultura, Roma, 1975, pp. 123 ff.

Chapter 3

1. J. Buchanan, "The Limits of Taxation," unpublished paper, presented at the Mont Pelerin Society meeting, Stanford, 1980, p. 2.

2. All articles of the Italian Constitution quoted herein are taken from the translation in N. Kogan, *The Government of Italy*, New York, 1962, *op. cit.*, pp. 188 ff. The translation is not Kogan's, but it is taken from United States Department of State, *Documents and State Papers*, Vol. I, No. 1, April 1948, pp. 46–63; it was made by Howard McGaw Smyth, Mediterranean Section, and Kent Roberts Greenfield, Chief Historian, Historical Division, Department of the Army.

3. This translation differs from that in Kogan, which reads: "No forced loan may be imposed on person or estate except on the basis of law." I believe that it is better to render "prestazione personale o patrimoniale" as "personal or patrimonial obligation," which consistently with the Italian text, is more general than "forced loan."

4. R. Nozick, *Anarchy, State, and Utopia*, New York, 1974, pp. 169–172.

5. F. Galgano (ed.), *La Costituzione Economica*, Padova, 1977.

6. V. Ottaviano, "Il governo dell'economia," in F. Galgano (ed.), *op. cit.*, pp. 185 ff.

7. *See*, for example, V. Falzone, F. Palermo, F. Cosentino (eds.), *La Costituzione della Repubblica Italiana*, A. Mondadori editore, 1976, p. 232; V. Carullo, *La Costituzione della Repubblica Italiana*, C. Zuffi editore, Bologna, 1950, p. 263. The account of the meeting of the second subcommittee is taken from Assemblea Costituente, Commissione per la Costituzione, Seconda Sottocommissione, *Resoconto Sommario*, pp. 419–422.

8. K. Wicksell, "A New Principle of Just Taxation," in *Classics in the Theory of Public Finance*, R. A. Musgrave and A. T. Peacock, eds., London, 1958. Wicksell's analysis is evidenced in R. E. Wagner and R. D. Tollison, *op. cit.*, p. 23.

9. *See*: Valerio Onida, *Le leggi di spesa nella Costituzione*, A. Giuffré editore, Milano, 1969, especially Chapter II, n.1.

10. For this, as for the whole history of the interpretation of the last paragraph of Art. 81, *see* the monumental work of V. Onida, *op. cit.*

11. L. Einaudi, *Lo scrittoio del Presidente (1948–1955)*, G. Einaudi, Torino, 1956, pp. 201–207.

12. Art. 74 says: "The President of the Republic, before promulgating a law, may by means of a message stating the reasons request a new decision of the Chambers. If the Chambers again approve a law, it must be promulgated." The two messages can be found in L. Einaudi, *Scritti economici, storici e civili*, R. Romano (ed.), A. Mondadori, 1973, pp. 715–716.

13. See V. Onida, *op. cit.*, pp. 17–22.

14. For the history of such a "process" of abandonment of the original interpretation of the last paragraph of Art. 81, see V. Onida, *op.cit.*

15. V. Onida, *op. cit.*

16. For this and the following arguments, *see* V. Onida, *op. cit.*, ch. VII, pp. 437–462.

17. Somewhere else, the author correctly criticizes interpretations of the constitutional principle based on the rejection of the politico-economic philosophy allegedly embodied in it. See, for example, pp. 160–161.

Chapter 4

1. For still another, recent empirical illustration in support of the quantity theory, *see* Robert E. Lucas, Jr., "Two Illustrations of the Quantity Theory of Money," *The American Economic Review,* December 1980, pp. 1005 ff.

2. For a recent work on the subject, *see* H. Geoffrey Brennan and James M. Buchanan, *Monopoly in Money and Inflation—The Case for a Constitution to Discipline Government,* Hobart Paper 88, I.E.A., London, 1981.

"I depend on POLICY REVIEW . . ."

**Representative Jack F. Kemp
(R.-New York)**

"A provocative journal—with its growing readership, it is very quickly becoming a publication that one should read."
> Senator Daniel Patrick Moynihan
> (D.-New York)

"A most stimulating reading experience."
> David Stockman
> (Director, Office of Management & Budget)

"In an age of endless 'analyses' that never quite find the point, POLICY REVIEW offers crisp, decisive essays on the great public questions of the day. Rarely have so many writers left so little to be said on so many issues."
> Joseph Sobran
> NATIONAL REVIEW

"A superior publication both in terms of content and design."
> Senator Orrin Hatch
> (R.-Utah)

When such a diverse group of political leaders agrees on the importance of one magazine, people take notice. It's no wonder that *Policy Review* is fast becoming the most widely discussed quarterly in America.

Policy Review is published by The Heritage Foundation, America's leading conservative public policy research institute. That explains its sound and timely analysis of both domestic and foreign affairs—a combination offered by no other conservative quarterly.

Recent issues of *Policy Review*, for example, have included articles on such topics as the Polish Crisis, Pornography, Affirmative Action, Contraception,

Energy, Counterintelligence, and the Environment—written by top experts from across the country and around the world.

Edited by John O'Sullivan, a former editorial writer for London's Daily Telegraph, *Policy Review* is known for its lively style and unpredictable controversy.

Find out for yourself why so many Washington policy-makers agree that *Policy Review* provides sound analysis of legislative issues, plus a wide range of policy alternatives—and a lively and provocative style.

Take advantage of our money-back guarantee and subscribe today.

PUBLISHED BY

The Heritage Foundation

Policy Review

513 C Street, N.E.
Washington, D.C. 20002

☐ Yes, I want to try *Policy Review*. Please enter a one-year subscription (4 issues), starting with the current issue. I understand that if I am not completely satisfied after receiving the first issue, I will receive a full refund.

☐ Enclosed is my $15 check for a 1 year subscription.

Please charge to my ☐ MasterCard ☐ VISA ☐ American Express ☐ Interbank # _____
(MASTERCHARGE only)

Credit Card No. _____ Exp. Date _____

Name _____

Address _____

City _____ State _____ Zip _____

Signature _____

RO1